MARRIAGES

AND

FAMILIES

ENRICHMENT THROUGH COMMUNICATION

Edited by

Sherod Miller

SOCIAL WORK COURSE
LINCOLN

 SAGE PUBLICATIONS *Beverly Hills / London* 1975

The material in this publication originally appeared as a special issue of SMALL GROUP BEHAVIOR (Volume 6, Number 1, February 1975). The Publisher would like to acknowledge the assistance of the special issue editor, Sherod Miller, in making this edition possible.

For information address:

SAGE PUBLICATIONS, INC.
275 South Beverly Drive
Beverly Hills, California 90212

SAGE PUBLICATIONS LTD
St George's House / 44 Hatton Garden
London EC1N 8ER

Printed in the United States of America

International Standard Book Number 0-8039-0569-6

Library of Congress Catalog Card No. 75-27012

FIRST PRINTING (this edition)

CONTENTS

FAMILY LIFE EDUCATION—A PERSPECTIVE ON THE EDUCATOR

VIRGINIA M. SATIR
Palo Alto, California

If there is a key word in this article I would have to say it is "human." It is the lack of humanness that I believe has contributed so heavily to the world's problems, and it is that very humanness which is such an essential and integral part of family life education as I see it.

Today it is possible to hear people saying with a sense of urgency that we need more and better family life education. Much of this concern probably is related to the increasing threat of the breakdown of the modern family, the evidence of which we can see all around us. Perhaps more of the concern is related to desperate attempts to avoid personal or social catastrophes. Probably at least as much concern has to do with people knowing somewhere within themselves that they could get more out of their lives as family members if only they knew how.

These days anyone who looks even remotely as if he might have anything to offer along the line of greater marital happiness, better parent-child relationships. and a more fulfilling life is likely to get an audience. The need is that great. The time is right now for giving priority to this need, and developing new models for family life education programs. People are our only resources. People run the world. And the way it is now, this world doesn't seem to fit too well for many of us. It seems to me that we had better direct more energy and attention to what really *human* human beings are so that we can have a more human world.

All people are born little and their education for being human is in the hands of their families. The family seems, then, the logical place to start. We have the need, we have the climate, we have people who want the education, and fortunately, we have people who are willing to offer themselves as leaders in taking on this difficult job.

At this time in our human history we have access to mountains of information, relating to human beings, which has been gleaned from all kinds of research, observation, and individual experience that has been accumulating for thousands of years. Some pieces of information reinforce others, some build on others, and still other pieces of information are in contradiction and seem unrelated. Most of these pieces have been translated into ways of thinking, feeling, and treating ourselves as human beings. For example, until recently good child-rearing practice meant keeping a rigid schedule for a child. He was fed by the clock instead of by his stomach. The aim was to help him develop adjustment within himself to the outside world. It was a way of socializing the child by disciplining his insides so that he could meet the expectations of the outside. In actuality, it was a way of putting his human part in a straitjacket and telling him that his humanness did not count—that what counted was how he could deny, destroy, or ignore everything about himself except what was acceptable to the outside. One of the difficult problems is deciding what is relevant in that fund of available information about human understanding. The family life educator has a great deal from which to choose. The name family life education implies a process of teaching and learning. The questions of learning what, for what, and why, immediately come into focus.

My admittedly oversimplified responses are really methods to learn more about being a *human* human being, so that the quality of all human life can be enhanced. Up to now, our society produces too much isolation, alienation, pain, destruction, and wasted human beings. Something has been wrong with the way we have approached training for humanness. For years we spent more money on raising pigs than we did on raising children. Maybe we still do.

Having come this far, another set of questions arises. Who can do the teaching? What is necessary to be taught? And how is it to be done?

The rest of this article will be devoted to my ideas relevant to these questions. I will proceed by giving an answer to the first question posed in the preceding paragraph: "Who can teach family life education?"

TEACHING FAMILY LIFE EDUCATION

I would look for a person who is fully knowledgeable about the literal development of human beings from birth to death, who understands what humanness is and what it means, who is experienced in the practice of his own humanness, who can listen to and comment on anything, who enjoys his own life and those who are close to him, who has a highly developed sense of humor, who understands group and family process and family system, who believes that people can learn at any age, who finds learning and growing exciting, who is practical in family matters, who is willing to experiment and be dramatic, who is patient, who feels himself to be intimately and consciously a part of a universal life force, and above all, who is congruent. I do not believe any one degree exists that requires this kind of preparation.

Reading the preceding paragraph might well frighten off anyone. These could seem like superhuman requirements, and indeed, they might be if we judged them by our usual achievement standards. But they are not if we think of them in terms of humanness. Everyone might not agree with me, but I believe they are achievable. Family life education is a very important undertaking and requires the very best in preparation.

I believe that people learn best in a clear, trusting, supporting, honest, alive, stimulating, emotional, and intellectual context. The teacher is the initiator and the model for developing this context.

I think that successful family life education can result in eventually changing the way the young are reared so that they grow up living their lives more humanly. They will then find more joy in family members, each and together, with the family learning how to become a source for greater stimulation of growth for all its members. They will then accept new knowledge and be creative in applying it, feel inspired to keep learning and growing, feel an increase in personal competence and responsibility, have a greater appreciation of what it means to be human, and a willingness to experiment with practical management procedures. They will have confidence to design self-help methods, appreciating and acknowledging the positive and negative realities, and will develop creative and appropriate ways to cope with them; finally, they will feel excited about exploring what is new and different in themselves and in the world around them.

Obviously what I have said so far represents what I have learned up to this point, which in the main has come from trying to make more sense and meaning out of my own life. My points related particularly to the outcomes of some of my struggles in being a *daughter,* one to a mother and one to a father, a *sister* to both sister and brother, a *wife, daughter-in-law, sister-in-law, mother, mother-in-law,* and *grandmother.* These all are family labels which many people wear at different times in their lives, just as I have. My first name remained the same regardless of the label, yet sometimes "me" and my label did not match too well. I have since discovered that this is a condition in which many others find themselves. My role is not the same as "me," but many people seem to behave as if it were so. For instance, after one becomes a "mother" she is no longer a "person."

The second source came as a result of choosing a life work which had to do with using myself to help other people, first as an elementary and secondary school teacher, and then as a psychotherapist with individuals and still later with families. Here my job meant I had to find some way to help people with their pain and their problems. And the way to do it lay in helping them discover the humanness and live with it.

The third source came through my efforts to teach other people to treat families.

The fourth came when I looked at the experiences of the first three and found the phenomenon common to all of them. This was when I began to see where education for being human came in. For example, I began to see that every time two people got together, there was a chance for differing. This was not because the two disliked one another, but simply because we are all unique, and if we are faithful to our uniqueness and are honest with ourselves and others, differences are bound to appear. I had felt and heard others say that the way to handle difference was to stamp it out, particularly since "only unloving people had differences."

Looking at difference as bad and stamping it out is very, very different from seeing it as a natural human aspect that is acceptable and can be used constructively. There is a great difference between dealing with something by stamping it out and acknowledging it and finding new uses for it. The question is not whether or not there are differences. The question is what are they and how can they be used? If this is a process that every human being experiences, then we can teach it.

There is a fifth source which has to do with looking and exploring areas not generally associated with behavior, such as space, time, position, color, air, light, and sound. How do these elements affect us? What can we learn that will make it possible to use these elements creatively?

The sixth source that has contributed to my position has to do with the thousands of people I have known who live in all parts of the world and in many settings doing various things—colleagues, students, people who came for help, chance acquaintances, friends, and family. The same phenomena kept coming up over and over again. Communication— how people make meaning with one another, the concept of self-worth, how people feel about themselves, their rules, how much of their humanness they permit themselves, links to society, how they connected with and influenced society, and how they were relating to a universal life force. There are kinds of communication that make relationships enjoyable and nurturing and there are kinds that do not. Every human being has a feeling about his worth. If one feels unworthy, his behavior will reflect that. The question is: how can self-worth be enhanced? There are emotional rules that stymie growth and there are those that stimulate it. How can we find rules that stimulate it? There are ways to link with the outside that nurture and there are ways that inhibit. How can we establish this link? Everyone is somehow connected to a source of life. How do we find that connection? How is it manifested?

I think we can teach communication that nurtures people, that we can teach rules which free them to grow, that we can teach an ability to achieve a heightened sense of self-worth, satisfying ways to cope with the outside, and a greater appreciation of their connection with a universal life force. We do not have to wait until people develop symptoms when we are in the process of repair, which is commonly called therapy. If we want to, through good family education we can enrich and prevent through education. Then we will not need as much repair. I believe that these concepts form the foundations for family education, and it is with them that the family life educator needs to concern himself. This will be an upstream effort for him as far as society is concerned, so he needs to feel pretty sure of his direction.

No baby comes into this world equipped with a "bag of directions" of how to grow and develop. What he learns depends upon what his parents believe are the "right" ways for him to function. We must not forget that. Whatever we are today, however we have changed, we still began with the basic learnings of our babyhood. The thread from then to now runs as surely as did the umbilical cord from our mothers to us in the womb.

CONCLUSION

Today, 1975, as we look back and around, and judging by the abundant presence of human misery, depression, alienation, and violence expressed in suicide, crime, alcoholism, drug addiction, physical and mental illness, we have reason to question what we have learned about being human.

I believe that no parent wants to teach his child how to be inhuman. Yet this is the result with so many of us that we cannot ignore it. Everyone I meet longs for a more human world. Why is it that so many of us do not have it? I think much of the answer lies in the meaning of the word "human." We are just beginning to know what it means. Most people I meet are far more concerned about being good and right and are trying hard not to be bad and wrong. In many places we call this civilizing people. Many people I have known who are both "good and right" have committed suicide, become alcoholics, or have become violent. We teach that love is a desirable expression of human beings. We talk a lot about it, but why is it that there is so little expression of it?

I think it is because as children we are asked to focus so much upon being right and good, on seeking approval and avoiding disapproval, that we learn very little about what it means to be human. Maybe it is much better to tell your mother that you are angry with her when you are, than to stuff back your rage because you cannot talk back to your mother.

From a human point of view, anger is a human aspect, an unpleasant one to be sure, but still human. Anger is felt physiologically, experienced emotionally, and interpreted intellectually. What kind of learning does it take for one to be willing to accept this and for everyone else to accept its presence? What kind of teaching is necessary to learn the many ways that anger can be used constructively? From the good-and-right point of view, anger is bad—wrong, and therefore it must be eliminated.

It is because of these long-held beliefs that we need training courses for leaders. If we recognize that there are a group of skills, a body of knowledge, and philosophy, and a process involved in teaching family life education, we will develop centers to do this.

To date, there are too few formal teaching programs which are set up primarily to prepare people to teach family life education. From my point of view, it needs to be an integral part of every kindergarten, elementary, and secondary school with a status equally as high as reading. This is really education for being human, and it has the highest priority. Without developing our people more fully and more humanly, the time might not be too far away when it will no longer matter whether or not we read, because we will not be around to do it.

A MODEL FOR COUPLES
How Two Can Grow Together

JOHN J. SHERWOOD
Graduate School of Industrial Administration
Purdue University
JOHN J. SCHERER
Leadership Institute of Spokane
Spokane, Washington

"Hello, I understand you're a marriage counselor. Well . . . you see . . . I'm really confused and upset right now. I'm not exactly sure why, but I think it began about a year ago when my husband and I first came here. Fred was enrolled as a graduate student. We had been dating and even lived together for a year before we both graduated from college. Those were really fun times. We used to spend a lot of time together. My husband treated me like I was someone very special and I thought he was just great. We had a lot of friends. Something was always happening. It was one of the happiest times of my life. Then we came to graduate school. The first week or so we were here Fred spent quite a few nights at the lab or at the library, but I didn't think much about it. In fact, I thought, 'Well I guess that's what it means to be a grad student'. But then, it got worse and worse. I mean nothing changed, and after a semester and a half, he still spends five or six nights a week at the lab. The only time I see him is when we eat breakfast and when he occasionally blows through for supper, because now he frequently eats supper at the lab. I don't know what to do. When I try to talk to him about it, he says, *'Dear, you don't understand. Everyone has to play by the same rules as everyone else and that's the way it is. Things will be different later—but now it's seven days a week, 24 hours a day or else people say you're not committed, and people who aren't committed simply don't get Ph.D.'s. This is just a highly competitive situation. As soon as I get my Ph.D., things will be better. You'll see—everything will be the way it used to be!'* I understand the pressure he is under and I believe him when he says things will be better, but I've had it! I don't know what to do. I still love him. I've thought about leaving. I just can't keep on this way. What can I do?"

Does Linda's story sound familiar? Anyone who has done any counseling or who has been a good neighbor or a good listener can write a similar scenario. Two people are attracted to each other, fall in love, get married, and somewhere in the first year or so of marriage things go sour. It seems almost inevitable that the realities of marital living do not meet our expectations. Most people who report this kind of experience are not emotionally disturbed; they are emotionally healthy people. They have not had any severe crisis in their lives. They simply live together as husband and wife and trouble seems to materialize out of nowhere. In recent years various experts have pointed to several rising indices, such as divorce rates, births outside of marriage, and adoptions by singles, and have raised questions about the viability of the institution of marriage as we have known it in this culture. We do not want to address that issue here, but what is clear to us is that what happens in a marriage today is no longer simply two people attempting to fulfill expectations established for them by others—e.g., society, parents, or *Good Housekeeping.* A marriage is more than ever a consequence of the dynamic interplay of the unique and changing needs, expectations, and *skills* of the two parties themselves.

We have a set of concepts that have proven useful in helping people like Linda and Fred understand how they got where they are—and more importantly—how to change their relationship so that it is more responsive to their changing needs. These concepts are put together in the form of a theoretical model, which we call "preventive maintenance for couples." Couples find when they begin using the model to view their relationship, they develop a new awareness about what happens between people when they live or work together. In addition, the model suggests new skills that help them "clean the slates" and maintain healthier, livelier, more expansive growing relationships.

Persons using the model learn (once again) that there is nothing as practical as a good theory (Lewin, 1951).

THE MODEL: PREVENTIVE MAINTENANCE FOR COUPLES

The model describes how relations between persons are established and become stabilized so there is continuity over time and how change can enter the system. The model is cyclical and it includes several phases:

(1) Sharing information and negotiating expectations. Every relationship, even the most casual one, begins with gathering data or information (the word, dating, itself sounds suspiciously like collecting data). As two people get to know each other, they learn things about the other's likes and dislikes, attitudes and opinions, and their characteristic behaviors. Furthermore, each learns a little about the other's view of himself or herself and something of his or her world view. While this data collection process is never formalized, our hunch is that even after a first date it would be possible for each party to make a rather lengthy list of things they learned about the other in the course of the initial encounter. In fact, they are not likely to have subsequent dates unless each is satisfied that the other possesses certain attributes which are important to him or to her (or unless the probabilities of that are sufficiently high).

While this information is being collected and shared another important and very subtle event takes place. The two people exchange and negotiate expectations each has for their relationship. (Others, such as Goffman, 1956: 162;

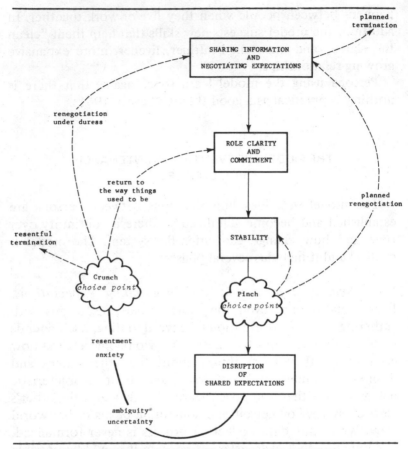

Figure 1: PREVENTIVE MAINTENANCE MODEL FOR COUPLES

1961: 105-132; Thibaut and Kelley, 1959: 21-25; and Blau, 1960, have written extensively on this process.) "I can expect her to be serious when we are alone and to kid around a lot when we're with her sister." "As for myself, I am a little hesitant to disagree with her, because she won't stop arguing until I admit she has a good point." While these expectations which each has for the other (and about oneself) are usually implicit and unspecified, the more information which is shared, the more likely the expectations will also be discussed and become mutual.

A useful illustration of what this is all about is found in comparing Greek and Hebrew concepts of knowing. In the Greek perspective, you "know" something only insofar as you are detached from it. Your task is to gather information about the person or object as it exists apart from you. The worst possible thing you could do would be to get attached or involved emotionally with the thing that is being known, as this only contaminates your knowledge and distorts your ever knowing it. The Hebrew concept of knowing is quite different. It is impossible to know anything without having a relationship with it. This method of knowing, then, is to move toward an intense involvement with the thing or person. So, what we often have in early dating is a shift from an initial Greek way of knowing (e.g., "Man, look at that bod!" or "Gee, I really like the way he smiles.") to more of a Hebrew perspective (e.g., "I like the way I feel when I am with him. I am comfortable and at peace with myself.").

What building a relationship really means is exchanging sufficient information so that the behaviors of both parties are more or less predictable, and uncertainty is reduced to an acceptable level.

(2) Role clarity and commitment. When expectations have been sufficiently shared and clarified, there is a growing clarity about the role each is to play in the relationship. "Oh, I see how I need to be with Fred to make this thing work." "Now I see what it means to be in a relationship with Linda." The implication is not that roles are phony. Quite the contrary. We all have many facets, all of which are us. The task of building a relationship is to discover which parts of us are the most comfortable in the particular relationship and then to share the expectations each person has for the other. As roles become clearer, then commitment becomes possible. The parties say, "Yes," at least tentatively, to the relationship.

As expectations are mutually understood and found acceptable or desirable, the two people find themselves moving toward some commitment to one another. Each person's role is becoming rather comfortably defined. Each knows for the most part what is expected of him/her, and for the most part each knows what he or she can expect from the other. As two people become more intimately involved, they frequently report feeling comfortable with one another. They also become more aware of the clarity and the predictability that each has about the role they are to play with the other. The strength of each individual's commitment and the range of behavior encompassed by their roles are both measures of the importance of this particular relationship. The more important the relationship, the more evidence of commitment is required and the more behaviors—including attitudes and values—are embraced by the role expectations. With commitment comes stability and continuity.

(3) Stability. When there is commitment to a set of shared expectations, these expectations govern the behavior of the two parties and provide stability in their relationship—that is, for the most part you do what I expect of you and for the most part I do what you expect of me. The couple's energies are now available for other things, since their relationship is sufficiently predictable that it no longer requires sustained attention. Therefore, they can also enjoy the satisfaction of being productive in addition to the pleasures their relationship brings them. The couple has a past, and they appear to be headed somewhere. The relationship has momentum, and it can sustain bumps in the road without disintegrating as it might have done at earlier points. Each has the feeling that the other person can be counted on to be there, and to be there even when things get rough.

Commitment to a set of shared expectations then governs behavior during a period of stability and productivity—but invariably, sooner or later, one of the persons is certain to feel pinched by the relationship (Blau, 1967; Homans, 1961).

(4) Pinch. A pinch is a sense of loss of freedom within one's current role and is a signal of the possibility of an impending disruption in the relationship. A person feeling a pinch would probably not call it a problem, but rather it is a hunch that something is just not right in his or her relationship with the other. A pinch is often described by a statement such as, "If things keep going this way, if he keeps doing that, I don't know what I'll do."

> "What's wrong, Linda? Are you and Fred having problems?" *"Oh no, no, he's been at the lab every night this week, but that's the only way he's going to get his Ph.D."* "I'll bet that makes you angry." *"No, but if it keeps up, I'll be at my wits end."*

A pinch is a choice point, since it is a glimmering of awareness of discomfort in one of the parties in the marriage, and it is connected to some specific behavior of the partner. With persons not accustomed to listening to their own feelings, a pinch may go unnoticed. But even if a pinch is noticed, quite frequently trouble often follows. Here is why: we are trained *not* to share our pinches. "Don't say anything to upset him/her." "Whatever you do, don't rock the boat." "If I tell her about this, it will only bother her." "Things have gone so well, I hate to tell him and cause trouble." When a young, married person feels a pinch, the first thing he wants to do with that uncomfortable feeling is pack it away in his own style—either under the rug, in his gunny sack, or whatever other handy way he has learned to distort or deny his own feelings in order to placate others and thereby avoid suspected trouble.

But there is irony here. In the very act of trying to avoid more difficult conflict, the person who hides his pinch often makes a much more serious problem more likely. If the behavior by the other person which led to the pinch continues, the pinch will not go away, and the conflict within the person feeling pinched is heightened and heightened until he is no longer able to cope with the discomfort the interaction now causes him. This immediately moves the relationship into a critical incident—a disruption of the previously shared expectations about how each is to behave.

(5) Disruption. Disruption occurs because of a violation of expectations by one or both of the parties or because of external intrusion into their relationship. Common examples of disruption which are external in origin are: the first child born into your marriage, losing your job, winning a lottery, moving into a new home (especially if one or more parents join you). The first child is a good example of how a new input into a relationship is likely to lead to the violation of previously established expectations—e.g., "What do you mean I should change the baby!"; "How come you're always so tired!"; "It's your turn to get up!" Disruptions may also be internal in origin, such as the sharing of information which was not made available earlier when expectations were being negotiated—e.g., "I know I *said* I liked your mushroom omelette, but I'm saying something different *now!*" People also change as a consequence of new experiences and education—"I just learned that Elizabeth's husband helps with the dishes!"

The event that gives rise to a disruption may be something that has happened a hundred times before. To return to our previous example, Fred gets up after supper to leave for the lab as he has for the last semester, and out-of-the-blue Linda angrily shouts: "This is it. I've had it. No more of this running off to the lab. This is the last straw." Fred is puzzled. He looks around and says, "What did I do? What's going on? I always leave for the lab at 6:30 right after supper." What had happened for Linda was that an earlier pinch was now becoming painfully clear to her. A significant expectation was not being met in her marriage: the expectation that, "my husband and I will spend a lot of time together." Once a critical incident and the subsequent disruption have occurred, it immediately throws the relationship over to the left side of the diagram (see Figure 1). Couples at this point report feelings of uncertainty, ambiguity, and confusion. "Gee, Fred, what's wrong?" "I don't know. I'm not sure, but things are really coming apart. I don't understand what it is." This then gives way to anxiety, sometimes fear, but almost always, resentment—toward the other person and probably toward one's self as well.

Now the two people are at an important choice point in their marriage, for it is at a moment of disruption that creative change can enter their relationship. They have basically three alternatives.

RESPONDING TO DISRUPTION

As shown in the diagram, a couple can respond to disruption in three rather different ways: (1) they can take the disruption into account and change (renegotiation); (2) they choose not to change and attempt to continue doing things the way they always have been by returning to "the way things used to be" (premature reconciliation); or (3) they can terminate their relationship. We will examine each of these options in some detail.

First, they can renegotiate their expectations. New information now enters their marriage, and they can renegotiate their expectations to bring them closer to the realities provided by the newly available information. The paradox is that the very moment the relationship is most open to change there are strong inhibiting forces working to return to "the way things used to be," because of anxiety accompanying the uncertainty which pervades the relationship at the time it is in a state of disruption (Lanzetta, 1955; Korchin et al., 1957).

When a disruption of expectations occurs, uncertainty follows—because I can no longer depend on your doing what I expect of you, and my own role is also unclear to me. With uncertainty, the parties become anxious. This anxiety is uncomfortable. Furthermore, at least one of the partners is probably angry. The quickest and surest way to reduce that anxiety and avoid that anger is for the relationship to return once again to "the way things used to be." This is the second alternative available to the couple. Fred comes home from the lab. Linda rushes to meet him at the door and says, "Dear, I'm so sorry about what I said earlier. Let's just forget about it. Let bygones be bygones. I know how important your work is to you and I understand. It's okay. Come in, let's have a glass of wine and forget about what happened."

The second alternative, whereby the couple attempts to return to their prior relationshp without talking about their expectations for one another, is a popular one. It is often a ritualized commitment to prior expectations, such as an apology, kiss, or embrace, without admitting the new information which gave rise to the disruption in the relationship. This new information could form the basis for discussion and change (renegotiation) of the expectations governing the relationship. However, the marriage remains closed to change when the parties deal with the uncertainty and anxiety produced by disruption by returning to the original level of sharing expectations without renegotiation— for example, the pledge, "it won't happen again," or the admonition, "don't let it happen again," or the reaffirmation of the way things used to be, "I love you" or "I'm sorry, I was wrong, everything is now okay . . . nothing is changed!" (Postman and Bruner, 1948; Hermann, 1963). This is premature reconciliation because it does not permit the new information which is now available to influence the couple's relationship.

It is during the period of disruption, when the parties are uncertain about their roles and the future of their relationship and are therefore anxious, that the system must be held open if change is to enter. If new information is allowed to enter the relationship and is treated in a problem-solving way, it can provide the basis for renegotiating the expectations governing the relationship. The newly renegotiated expectations are therefore more likely to be in line with the current realities of the situation, and once commitment occurs, the period of stability is likely to be more enduring before the next ensuing disruption.

If the parties share this model as a part of their language and their mutual expectations, these concepts are likely to help them by increasing their tolerance for the uncertainty and the accompanying anxiety which surround their relationship while expectations are held open during renegotiation. Through continued use of these concepts, the behavioral skills of the parties also increase, thereby facilitating the renegotiation process.

Understanding the renegotiation process and building the skills to help move through such trying times is essential both to maintain a satisfying marriage and to permit the two parties to grow. This is because it is assumed that disruption is inevitable, only the period of stability and our coping styles vary, because (a) information about ourselves and our actual reactions to the other person are never completely shared during the initial period when expectations are negotiated; and (b) people change with time and experience, and they learn from contacts with others outside the marriage. Where couples accept the inevitability of change and disruption and understand that their relationship is never "settled and worked out once and for all," while disruptions will remain uncomfortable and anxious they are no longer viewed as signs of imminent disaster. Just as Bach and Wyden (1969) suggest that fighting can be viewed as a source of new information, and therefore one can learn to fight productively and to recognize destructive fighting, so it is with disruptions of expectations. People can learn to treat disruptions as opportunities for new information to enter their relationship, and therefore, as times for change.

The theory predicts that disruption without renegotiation leads to an increasing frequency and intensity of disruptions. When each disruption is not treated as a new source of information and a new opportunity for adjustment of expectations and change, but rather as a disagreeable state that cannot be tolerated due to the urgency to return to "the way the things used to be," then the source of the disruption is never satisfactorily remedied, improved, or even ameliorated. If the difficulty in the relationship is never addressed directly, it is likely to persist and add to the intensity of future disruptions precipitated by new problems entering the relationship. The more inflexible the marriage, the more likely a final disruptive event will be explosive and destructive. Such a relationship is likely to have a resentful termination, which is destructive to all the parties involved.

The third alternative is, of course, to terminate the relationship. It is a popular option, because there are several ways to terminate a relationship. One can depart physically, get a legal separation, or a divorce. There are other ways to terminate while still continuing to be physically present. Drugs, like alcohol and marijuana, are used by some persons to avoid the painful, authentic encounter with the other person required to work on their relationship. Others use prescription drugs. It would be difficult to prove, but our hunch is that part of the high rate of alcoholism and drug abuse among middle-aged, married men and women may be an avoidance of the difficulties of dealing openly with the conflicts of marriage.

Another way to terminate the relationship, while remaining legally married, is to become involved with another person. This is a choice to shift your commitment elsewhere by transferring energy away from a relationship filled with pain to one where you are more comfortable. One's lover is especially attractive in contrast to the ways things are at home. As was said earlier, the theory predicts that disruption without renegotiation leads to an increasing frequency and intensity of disruptions, however, the intensity of future disruptions is not likely to be increased when difficulties in the marriage are handled by reducing commitment to the relationship. In this case, an apparent return to "the way things used to be" is actually a withdrawal of commitment. Over time such a strategy leads to an atrophied relationship. To use Ingmar Bergman's phrase, the marriage becomes a "comfortable disaster."

Whenever disruption occurs, the possibility of terminating the relationship is always an alternative solution. Termination is more likely to be a constructive, problem-solving solution based on new information when it is a consequence of renegotiation (see the planned termination option illustrated in Figure 1). Termination is more likely to be destructive to one or both of the parties, when one or more of the following are present: (1) the disruption is unexpected and explosive, (2) the relationship is rigid and inflexible, or (3) the parties have little or no prior experience in renegotiating adjustments to changing conditions.

Let's go back to the pinch again.

PLANNED RENEGOTIATION

The model states that relationships cycle through (1) the sharing of information and negotiation of expectations, through (2) role clarity and commitment, to (3) stability and productivity, to (4) disruption and the possibility of renegotiation and therefore change. It has also been shown that it is difficult to hold things open for renegotiation because of the uncertainty and anxiety that prevails at that time. These concepts then provide a way to introduce controlled change by anticipating disruption and renegotiating expectations in advance of disruption. This is known as planned renegotiation, and it is based on learning to act on a pinch.

An example of a pinch which raises the possibility of renegotiation is found in Mary's statement, "When Bob told me how happy he was that hunting season is almost here, I felt annoyed." Bob was confused at Mary's annoyance, answering "But you knew I love to hunt when we got married!" The stage is now set. Mary and Bob can further explore this source of potential difficulty in their relationship by sharing additional information, and perhaps, by renegotiating the expectations each has for the other; or (2) they can allow this opportunity (Mary's pinch) to pass by smoothing over Mary's annoyance and Bob's surprise by assuming that "things will work themselves out." Just as Mary had two choices, to share her annoyance with Bob or to let it pass; so the couple has two options, to talk further and explore this potential source of difficulty or to let it pass. Since a pinch is not a disruption—even when it is shared with the other party—it is easy for the couple to allow Mary's annoyance to pass relatively unnoticed.

Should Mary and Bob choose to pursue the hunch that there is something of importance to Mary's pinch, the surest way for them to make progress in beginning to renegotiate some of their expectations for each other is for them to understand and share what each wants from the other and what each fears from the other. As long as their conversation is about issues, such as hunting, a shootout is more likely to develop, which then often requires a winner and a loser. When both parties can share their wants and fears, they can see where they are apart and where they hold expectations in common. This makes renegotiation a more likely event.

BOB	*MARY*
"I want to be free to hunt whenever I wish, but I also want to be close to you and to be loved by you. When you get angry about my hunting, I feel you moving away from me."	"I want to be around you more to feel as if I count with you. I feel like I am nothing to you when you choose hunting over me. I want to have some influence with you."
"I fear that you will lose interest in me, or even leave me all alone,	"My fears are that I don't really count with you, that you don't

and that if you ever get control, love me, and that there is no you'll stop me from hunting way for me to influence you." altogether."

Bob and Mary are talking about their expectations—what they want and what they fear. A new set of relationship dynamics is now possible. Mary and Bob need to be able to work out how much hunting is too much (for Mary) and enough (for Bob), and perhaps, how Bob can signal Mary's importance to him even when he chooses to go hunting. While Mary may never like it when Bob is away hunting, once she realizes that she has some influence over Bob and that she is important to him, she may get angry less often and withdraw her love less frequently—and this may make it easier for Bob to indicate how much he cares for her, even while choosing to go hunting.

What would have happened if Mary had chosen not to share her annoyance with Bob? Quite frequently, the answer is that not much would have happened at that point in time. The couple would be setting the stage for a disruption sometime in the future. Sometimes people are able to treat their pinches as new information, and therefore, as opportunities to renegotiate aspects of their relationship. Sometimes a pinch gives rise to blaming the other: then this is experienced as an attack, which leads to defensive responses. For instance, Bob might experience Mary's concern about the amount of time he spends hunting as a charge against him; if so, he might respond defensively and tell her that she simply does not understand. The couple would then begin moving toward a disruption in the future. But, we have found when couples have this model explained to them along with the following strategy that they are able to share their pinches and work with them in ways that can be beneficial to their relationship.

The basic rules are these: (1) When one person feels a pinch, the other person also has a pinch. That is to say, when one member of a marriage is uncomfortable with the relationship, the relationship needs some immediate attention. The maintenance required may simply be sharing the pinch itself. This new information may be all that it takes. Once a pinch is shared, there needs to be (2) a *mutual* choice whether or not to work on this new information. If a couple then decides to work on the pinch, it is (3) discussed in terms of a problem to be solved (rather than a case to be prosecuted or a fight to be won) by changing expectations to take into account the new information which is now available to both parties. It is helpful to use the following kinds of statements in sharing, clarifying, and renegotiating expectations: "I want . . . "; "I wish you would . . . "; "I am afraid that . . . "; rather than charges, attacks, or accusations, such as "The trouble with you is . . . " or "If it wasn't for you . . . ," which raise defenses and bring on counterattack, distortion, or denial.

PEOPLE'S NEED FOR CONCEPTS

Where this simple model of how roles are established between two people and how they change is available to the couple and where they have skills in sharing their reactions to one another's behavior, talking about their feelings, and describing their relationship, change can be introduced in a controlled and fairly systematic way. Pinches are treated as sources of new information from which the couple can planfully renegotiate some of the expectations of their relationship.

Of course, the model also serves the purpose of making it clearly legitimate to talk about my expectations of you and my understanding of your expectations of me. Furthermore, the model shows the couple that the future is filled with change and that they must gear themselves to learn to incorporate change into their marriage. Disruptions are on the horizon. What varies is their timing and the skills we have to treat them as sources of new information upon which to build a more satisfying relationship with one another.

Renegotiation, of course, also takes place at times of disruption. These times are however more stressful, because of the uncertainty, anxiety, and anger, and also because concern with preserving the relationship becomes central. Couples often rightfully choose to seek counseling to help them through some of the more difficult disruptions in their marriage. Whereas for couples who learn to plan renegotiation around the new information that pinches produce for them, not only are emotions likely to be less intense and the pressure lower, but it is working on a problem, rather than preserving the relationship, which becomes central. It is the question: "What's going on?" versus "We'd better find a remedy or else . . . "

Both the model and the concept of planned renegotiation can thus become parts of the relationship—so that whenever I feel a pinch, that pinch is shared as a signal, and the question of renegotiation of expectations is raised. The parties thereby have more choice and more control over change. They are subject to fewer negotiations under fire, and they are less often victims of crises and pressures to return to "the way things used to be."

We believe people need concepts to guide their behavior. The theory underlying the concept of planned renegotiation is clear, simple, and straightforward. It is intended that the concepts become part of the language of a marriage. Persons can train themselves in the skills of planned renegotiation. It is important that people learn to detect pinches before disruptions develop.

One couple with whom we have used this model nicknamed it, "Pay me now or pay me later," after an advertisement which asserts that a small amount of time and money spent on maintenance at the first sign of car trouble saves a lot of time and money later when a major overhaul would be necessary.

Another illustration of the principle of preventive maintenance comes from experience on a destroyer in the navy. As the boilers work to move the ship through the water, carbon deposits occasionally build up inside the tubes, shrinking the size of the opening. To make sure the tubes do not close entirely thus putting the ship dead in the water, once every four hours or so a small portion of the steam used to drive the turbines and propel the ship is redirected through the tubes. The carbon is thereby removed and the tubes are cleared for effective work. Every relationship needs to pause regularly to "blow the tubes" or stand by to go dead in the water with a critical incident.

A pinch is felt by an individual, whereas a disruption is experienced by all parties involved in the relationship. It is therefore incumbent upon an individual who feels a pinch also to take responsibility for raising the question of renegotiation with the partner, rather than asserting that it is someone else's problem or responsibility. At the same time, it is important for people to understand that when they experience a pinch, this is going to make them anxious. When a pinch is shared and renegotiation considered, then others become anxious as well. People get anxious both because of the uncertainty which is introduced into the relationship, and because they are never sure whether they will personally be better off after the renegotiation is completed than they were before. When people work with this model, they learn that anxiety becomes controlled and tolerable when there is a commitment to problem-solving. There remains nevertheless a risk each time the relationship is opened for examination and change.

Can a relationship survive the growth of the partners? Can marriages survive women's liberation or other changes in roles or persons? Our answer is yes—with awareness, skill, and the guts to try to understand where you are and what changes will bring both partners into a more satisfying relationship with one another.

In the first few attempts at renegotiation within the model, people are simultaneously working on two problems: (1) trying out a problem-solving model and developing skills and procedures for its use, and (2) working on the pinch that gave rise to the renegotiation. Over time both skills and procedures develop, as does confirmation of the model and its usefulness to the parties involved (or its lack of usefulness).

In using the concepts of preventative maintenance for couples, people have more choice in their lives and are less likely to be victims of the way things used to be.

REFERENCES

BACH, G. R. and P. WYDEN (1969) The Intimate Enemy. New York: William Morrow.

BLAU, P. M. (1967) Exchange and Power in Social Life. New York: John Wiley.

——— (1960) "A theory of social integration." Amer. J. of Sociology 65. 550-553.

GOFFMAN, E. (1961) Encounters. Indianapolis: Bobbs-Merrill.

——— (1956) The Presentation of Self in Everyday Life. Edinburgh, Scotland: University of Edinburgh.

HERMANN, C. F. (1963) "Some consequences of crisis which limit the viability of organizations." Administrative Sci. Q. 8: 61-82.

HOMANS, G. C. (1961) Social Behavior: Its Elementary Forms. New York: Harcourt, Brace & World.

KORCHIN, S. J. et al. (1957) "Visual discrimination and the decision process in anxiety." AMA Archives of Neurology and Psychiatry 78: 424-438.

LANZETTA, J. T. (1955) "Group behavior under stress." Human Relations 8: 29-52.

LEWIN, K. (1951) Field Theory in Social Science. (D. Cartwright, ed.) New York: Harper.

POSTMAN, L. and J. S. BRUNER (1948) "Perception under stress." Psych. Rev. 55: 314-323.

SHERWOOD, J. J. and J. C. GLIDEWELL (1972) "Planned renegotiation: a norm-setting OD intervention," pp. 35-46 in W. W. Burke (ed.) Contemporary Organization Development. Arlington, Virginia: NTL Institute. (also available as Paper 338, Institute for Research in the Behavioral, Economic, and Management Sciences, Purdue University)

THIBAUT, J. W. and H. H. KELLY (1959) Social Psychology of Groups. New York: John Wiley.

WE CALL IT ACME

DAVID R. MACE
Behavioral Sciences Center
Bowman Gray School of Medicine

I once believed that, if only we could train enough professional counselors, we could cut back marriage and family failure rates to a level that our culture could comfortably tolerate. Acting on that belief, I have devoted most of my life to the development of marriage and family counseling, involving programs and projects in some sixty countries.

It was only when a heart attack stopped me in my tracks and gave me time to think that I saw at last the irrefutable logic of the old adage that prevention is better than cure. It became painfully clear that, as long as our interventions in marital and family dysfunction were remedial only, we would make only a limited impact on the state of family life in our culture as a whole. To wait until couples are in serious trouble is to choose the worst possible strategic ground for the application of our hard-won knowledge and skill. This seems eloquently demonstrated by the fact that we now have tens of thousands of highly skilled and dedicated professionals involved in marriage and family counseling—and the family is sinking deeper and deeper in a sea of trouble.

This is, of course, an oversimplification. Marriage and the family, like all ancient and honorable institutions, are in violent transition in contemporary society. Besides, not all marriages will work and some families are best disbanded. Yet when all allowances have been made, the fact remains that large numbers of men and women still want, expect, and hope for a happy and fulfilling marriage. Even the failure of a first marriage finds most of them ready to try again. Enduring dyadic intimacy has been a basic human quest throughout the entire span of recorded history. In legend and the arts alike, romantic love is a recurring theme.

How then, the question presented itself, can we provide married couples with the kind of preparation, guidance, and support that will maximize their chances of attaining the goal they so fervently desire? The logical answer was: "Enable them to develop such good relationships that they will keep out of serious trouble." The next question followed: "But *can* we do this?" The answer to this one was not so clear; but at least I believed we could do very much better than we have been doing—and that was a good enough reason to make a start.

I figured we had now enough knowledge to offer real help to married couples. In recent years we have been gathering useful new data about communication, about conflict resolution, about sexual adjustment; but we have not yet achieved much in the direction of making it dynamically available to couples. The average American couple are able to make no more use of our present knowledge of marital interaction than is the Indian peasant farmer able to draw on the resources of agricultural science. The result in both cases is the same—a miserable yield for much effort expended.

So, we had the resources. But how were we to make them available to couples? That was the toughest problem of all. The fact that finally emerged was so staggeringly illogical that at first I could hardly believe it. The sober truth is that married couples desperately want to have loving relationships, but fanatically resist attempts to enable them to get what they want! A more comprehensible way of saying this is that our culture exalts the concept of the happy marriage, and then builds in a series of roadblocks to make sure that very few couples achieve it!

The first roadblock is what Clark Vincent has called the "myth of naturalism." It says—"Anyone can make marriage work. You have all the built-in equipment. Just follow your instincts. Only an incompetent fool, a really deficient person, could fail in such a simple task." That is what the culture tells us. It is an unexamined prejudice that persists in the face of all evidence to the contrary. To admit you are having difficulties in marriage ranks as a humiliating confession of failure in an elementary human task.

The second roadblock is privatism. It is obviously related to the first. It says—"Marriage is very private, very personal. Whatever you do, don't ever talk to anyone else about what goes on inside your marriage." To a reasonable degree, this makes sense. There are all sorts of good reasons for taboos. But when a taboo is retained at an appalling cost, it must be reexamined. And this "intermarital taboo," as I have called it, is today doing far more harm than good. It is shutting married couples up together in lonely little boxes where in their fumbling ignorance they destroy the very things they most desire. They are allowed to break out and seek help only when so much havoc has been wrought that the counselors to whom they turn can often do little to repair the ravaged relationship.

A third roadblock is cynicism. You have to sharpen your wits to become aware of the extent to which we are cynical about marriage. Listen carefully, however, to the boisterous jokes, the snide remarks, the subtle innuendoes that pervade almost any discussion of marriage. Indeed, in ordinary social conversation marriage is hardly ever seriously discussed. It is openly or covertly ridiculed.

So what our culture is saying, in effect, is—"Only a fool would need to *learn* to be married, or would ask for help.

However, if you really *must* seek help, don't seek it till the situation is absolutely desperate. And it probably won't be any good anyway, because marriage is a grossly overrated institution."

The problem, therefore, is how to counteract these powerful cultural pressures. How can we get married couples to shed these gross misconceptions, and accept the true facts—that marriage is a deeply rewarding experience when you really make it work; that in order to do so we all need a great deal of training in very complex skills; and that most of us also need the help and support of other married couples in the process?

All this I came to see clearly. It presented a formidable task. Yet it was a task vitally important, because without good marriages you cannot have good families, and without good families you cannot produce the kinds of citizens who will shape good communities.

My wife and I, after about two years of thinking this through and talking it over with professionals and married couples, came up with the best answer we could find. We call it ACME. Spelled out, it is The Association of Couples for Marriage Enrichment. But the word ACME has its own appropriate symbolism. In Greek it means the highest peak to which you can climb.

A NATIONAL ORGANIZATION FOR MARRIED COUPLES

We decided to form a national organization of married couples, because we believed the only way to challenge the taboo was to meet it head-on. Most people have not considered the startling fact that never in the world's history, so far as I am aware, have married couples organized themselves in support of good marriage. Yet human beings are incurably gregarious, and in all but the strict taboo areas their natural instinct is to band together round a common interest. Photographers organize to promote photography, astronomers to promote astronomy, artists to promote art, musicians to promote music. Blacks have united, women have united, retired persons have united, to foster their shared interests. Married couples have organized for social, recreational, and religious purposes. They have even united in the PTA to promote their interests as parents. What they have never done is to unite to promote the cause most central to their welfare—the cause of good marriage. That is forbidden territory.

On that forbidden territory ACME has raised a small flag and calls on married couples to gather round it. We invite couples to support four objectives:

(1) to work for the enrichment of their own marriages. Our slogan is—"To work for better marriages, beginning with our own";

(2) to unite with other couples for mutual support by planning programs together for marriage enrichment;

(3) to initiate and support more adequate community services designed to help marriages;

(4) to improve the public image of marriage as a relationship capable of promoting both individual development and mutual fulfillment.

At this writing, ACME has been in existence less than a year. What has happened?

We have established a North American organization with national officers (all couples) and a national headquarters. We have secured encouraging support from all the principal professional organizations in the field of marriage and the family, from many concerned religious groups, and from a number of enlightened public figures. We have appointed State Representatives (again couples) in about half of the states. We have completed plans for a National Conference on Marriage Enrichment co-sponsored by eight national organizations in the field. We have made contact with groups all over the continent which are developing marriage enrichment programs of one kind or another, and which seem to reflect a genuine grass-roots movement to take marriage more seriously.

In two directions our progress has been slow. One is in the area of publicity. The mass media just are not interested, so we are obviously not news. The New York *Times* put a small notice of ACME's formation on the obituary page one morning, dropped it in a later edition to make room for the announcement of someone's death. Two leading free-lance writers have tried persistently and failed to secure any interest in an article for one of the national magazines. Two interviews written up for prominent daily papers never made it into print. A national newspaper called three times for information, finally printed nothing. No radio or TV program has shown the slightest interest in the idea of couples uniting in the interests of good marriage.

One other area of slow progress has been the recruiting of ACME members. All our assumptions about the taboo have been abundantly confirmed. Couples generally are very interested in ACME and curious about it. They often commend us for what we are doing. Some say we have a good idea. But when invited to join, they become evasive and make excuses. They say ACME appears to be an organization for perfect marriages, and they do not qualify. They say their marriages are all right, thank you, and they do not need our help. They say they will think it over, they do not have the time to devote to it, they cannot afford the $12 annual dues. A few tell us honestly that they could not face their children, their neighbors, their relatives, colleagues, or friends, because they would be mercilessly ridiculed for joining an organization to improve their marriages.

Nevertheless, couples are joining ACME in a steady trickle if not a swelling stream. Those who join tend to be unusually mature, purposeful couples who do not mind challenging the taboo. What is abundantly clear is that the whole idea of marital growth and enrichment is so new that most couples have as yet no frame of reference in which to see it in logical perspective. What we find, however, is that once they grasp the idea they become enthusiastic about it. Once an ACME chapter is established in a community, it grows steadily as member couples persuade their friends and neighbors that it is a sound idea.

We are therefore now convinced of two facts—that ACME will inevitably grow, and that it will inevitably grow slowly, through couple-to-couple advocacy. Our concern therefore is to develop what we already know to be the best means to promote that growth—couple group interaction.

RELAXING THE INTERMARITAL TABOO

The intermarital taboo has locked us into stereotyped patterns of thinking about marriage which are grossly inaccurate, just as our taboo on sex allowed a farrago of foibles and fallacies about human sexuality to dominate our thinking. The accepted view of marriage is that it is static—a state, or estate, brought about by the legal contract, which it is the duty of those concerned to preserve in a condition of stability or permanence. Our culture recognizes only two kinds of marriage—good and bad. All marriages are judged to be good when they start, and to continue to be good unless or until they are in such serious trouble that the couple seek counseling help or resort to divorce.

Once a group of couples are able to relax the taboo, however, they soon begin to see marriage quite differently. They discover that the average marriage is neither good nor bad, but a mixture of desirable and undesirable components. They realize that stability is an almost meaningless term, because the relationship between marriage partners is dynamic, fluid, constantly changing as they themselves change and as their life situation changes. They begin to perceive that the really important question about a marriage is whether the processes of change taking place in it represent upward growth or downward degeneration. They realize that

the guilty, problem-oriented attitude to the inevitable difficulties of dyadic adjustment is quite inappropriate, and that
the concept of overcoming obstacles together in a process of
mutual growth makes much better sense.

In other words, when groups of married couples, by
breaking the taboo, are able for the first time to see the
insides of each other's marriages, their whole perception of
marriage undergoes significant change. It is for this reason
that the marriage enrichment movement, with a few notable
exceptions, has found couple group interaction to be its most
valuable tool.

ACME, as a comprehensive national organization, recognizes all patterns of group interaction that demonstrably
produce marriage enrichment. We are continually studying,
comparing, and contrasting the available models to assess
their value. Let me report a few of our findings to date.

Broadly speaking, marriage enrichment groups either meet
for a continuous and intensive, shared experience (usually
over a weekend) or for a series of evening meetings once a
week. Within one or other of these contexts, we have
identified three models, graduated in terms of the depth of
group interaction which takes place.

First is the marriage encounter pattern, in which no group
interaction as such normally occurs. The action here is
confined to direct husband-wife confrontation, stimulated by
testimonies from the leader couples under the direction of
the attendant priest. However, the social and religious
support provided by the group plays an important role, and
there is no question that the intensive, supervised encounter
with each other is a most effective means of stimulating
couple growth and enrichment.

The second model is usually called a marriage communication lab. Normally this is a structured program which offers
preplanned content, covering areas of marriage which commonly cause difficulty—communication, decision-making, intimacy, sex, and so on. In this model extensive use is made of

exercises which facilitate dynamic interaction both at intra-couple and intercouple levels.

The third model is one which my wife and I have developed during the twelve years in which we have been leading marriage enrichment retreats. It involves a minimum of structure and no preplanning. The program is allowed to take shape around the expressed needs of the particular group of couples, the understanding being that there shall be no exchange of opinions, but only a sharing of experiences and an attempt by the group to understand and interpret them. Experiences are not reported directly to the group, but communicated as the marriage partners dialogue directly with each other.

There is abundant evidence of the effectiveness of all three models, and it will be some time before their comparative merits can be estimated.

What are the distinctive characteristics of marriage enrichment groups, as compared with other forms of group process?

First, it must be clearly understood that a group of married couples is not a group of individuals, and that the group dynamics involved differ significantly. What we are considering here is a group of subgroups, each of which is a preexisting and continuing social unit. This means greater complexity, because it includes intracouple and intercouple interactions, neither of which plays a significant part in groups of individuals.

Second, these are not therapy groups, for it is the general rule that the participation of couples with serious difficulties is strongly discouraged. This means that leadership of such groups can be successfully undertaken by carefully selected and trained nonprofessional persons. The evidence of their effectiveness is reassuring.

Third, the general consensus is that the best facilitators for such groups are married couples who play a fully participative role as members of the group, rather than the separate, authoritative role normally assumed by the therapist. There is much evidence that the leader couple serve as models for the couples in the group and are "adopted" as surrogate parents.

Fourth, because the objective is not therapy, these groups are not normally problem-oriented. The emphasis is on the growth concept and on the search for positive methods of moving ahead to new and more rewarding behavior patterns. Some clinicians who learn this are inclined to regard it as manifesting evasion of the real issues. Yet in fact, although therapy is not the goal, a surprising amount of effective therapy does incidentally take place.

Fifth, these are not encounter groups in the usual meaning of the term. They seldom employ confrontation tactics. Negative emotion is not deliberately envoked, though when it emerges, as it inevitably does, it is accepted with compassionate understanding. Care is usually taken, also, to make all active participation entirely voluntary. I can remember one retreat in which a particular couple, after the first introductions, chose to remain interested spectators throughout.

MARITAL GROUP INTERACTION

What processes occur in these group experiences? First, there is the relaxing of the taboo, which becomes possible through the building up of trust and the willingness of couples to make themselves vulnerable. This brings a state of relaxation and openness of the couples to each other. An immediate result is reassurance as couples realize that their supposedly unique difficulties are in fact shared by others. Cross-identifications then develop between couples with similar situations, who tend to get together for deeper sharing outside the group sessions. A great deal of modeling takes place as couples see how others have dealt with, and are dealing with, adjustments currently confronting them. All these processes build an atmosphere of strong mutual support among the couples, who often find themselves forming something like a loving family circle with the leader couple as parent figures. The bonds that unite a group are enduring. When members meet again later they immediately resume the close "family" relationship they experienced at the retreat, dropping the defense systems characteristic of normal social interaction patterns.

We find that these group experiences can bring about a remarkable degree of relational growth and change in a short period of time. The couple's perception of their interaction pattern rapidly gains accurate perspective. They are encouraged to formulate goals for mutual growth, and to take first steps in the direction of achieving them. They see the futility of self-defeating patterns and agree together to abandon them for more creative ways of interacting. This provides a powerful stimulus for continuing the process of change, and later contacts with couples who have really entered into the group experience almost invariably show that marriage enrichment has taken place. It seems that the retreat breaks log-jams and gets couples moving again in the direction of marital growth.

Of course some couples derive limited benefit. These are the ones who are resisting change and growth too stubbornly to be able to move. Or they are couples who have considerable pathology, and should never have come to a retreat. Such couples do get under the wire occasionally despite all our precautions. Sometimes one partner is ready for change but the other cannot cooperate. In some of these situations the leaders are able to refer the couples to professional help. Indeed, couples are often made aware of their need of marriage counseling through the group experience and later seek it.

Although marriage enrichment groups undoubtedly are powerful agencies for initiating change and growth, it would be unreasonable to see them as a wonder-working panacea. Poor patterns of marital behavior cannot be radically altered in the course of a weekend retreat or a few weeks of participation in a growth group. One of our main reasons for launching ACME was our awareness that the group experience is for most couples a very promising new beginning, but that this alone is not enough. It is true that the fall-out rates following couple groups appears to be far lower than for groups of individuals, because a social unit in which change has been initiated manifests greater momentum for continuity. But it is a fact that most current programs for marriage enrichment function on a one-shot basis, and this I would consider to be unsatisfactory. Worse still are programs which offer so-called "marriage enrichment" experiences of such short duration, so superficial, or so poorly led, that participating couples gain very little and conclude there is nothing more to it.

ACME's goals are long-term, and offering retreats and growth groups is only part of the program. True, we want our couples to have these experiences. But we want them also to become associated, through their local chapter, with other couples who are committed to work toward substantial realization of their own marital potential, and also to provide similar help and encouragement to other couples in their community.

Developing marital potential covers many areas of relationship, and our idea is that the ACME chapter should provide for all of them, combining with professionals to develop comprehensive services. This would mean training courses in couple communication, help in developing successful patterns of decision-making, conflict resolution, sex adjustment, and the like. Some of these services would be organized by the chapter for groups of couples, others would involve referral to marriage counselors and other professionals whose competence had been checked out. The scope of services offered could be widened where necessary to include contraception, natural childbirth, financial planning, real estate purchase, household management, parent effectiveness, and the like.

One of our long-term hopes is that the role of the marriage counselor can be shifted to an increasing emphasis on preventive rather than remedial intervention. Some day every sensible married couple will have their own marriage counselor, just as every sensible family now has its own physician and dentist; and they will go routinely for an annual marital check-up. Why not? The dentists have persuaded us to have our teeth preventively cared for, and surely we value our marriages as much as our teeth? This will mean a radical change in public opinion; yet no more so than has already occurred in the widespread acceptance of family planning, which at one time was bitterly opposed. As ACME develops, we shall ask member couples to volunteer to commit themselves to the annual marital check-up by way of setting an example to others.

It is also our intention to use ACME couples, when they are ready and willing, to help other couples in need. Through marriage enrichment groups we have come to realize the vast untapped potential that lies in the power of married couples to help each other, once the taboo has been relaxed. We think this can be very productively used.

For example, we are now experimenting with what we call extension growth groups. The concept is to enable two or three ACME couples to interact with perhaps three other couples who can benefit from close interaction with them. One form of this would be a marriage preparation group in which the other three were moving toward marriage. Because of the taboo, young people today have no opportunity to observe effectively working models of the new pattern of companionship marriage which is our emerging marital goal. In such an extension growth group, the engaging couples could observe how warm, loving relationships are achieved, and this could be a better learning experience for them than any other we are able to provide.

ACME couples could similarly be placed in groups with couples in difficulties before, during, or after marriage counseling, under appropriate professional supervision. There are other ways in which they could serve as counselors' aides. One possibility would be for ACME couples to man a "hot line" which a couple in a crisis situation could use to get immediate support, followed up by a meeting with an ACME couple and referral to appropriate professional help. Another possibility would be to move recently divorced persons into a group with several ACME couples, to support them in the postdivorce trauma, and to help them prepare for later remarriage. An experiment has already been carried out in organizing marriage enrichment groups for married men nearing the end of their prison terms and their wives, to prepare them for the difficult readjustments involved in their forthcoming reunion.

CONCLUSION

We call it ACME, and it beckons us to climb difficult peaks. Yet it is my conviction that the concept of marriage enrichment, with all its diverse implications, is one of the most hopeful grass-roots movements we have seen in a long time. It is directed toward the rehabilitation of the nuclear human relationship that is the foundation of the family, which in turn is the foundation of human society. Father Gabriel Calvo, the Spanish Catholic priest who founded Marriage Encounter, summed it up when he said—"We believe that helping a married couple to form a true community of love, a community open to the love of their children, and to the love of the whole society around them, is really working at the root of things."

NOTE

The only book about ACME is by David and Vera Mace, *We Can Have Better Marriages, If We Really Want Them* (Abingdon Press, 1974). ACME members receive a bimonthly newsletter. Four supplements on particular topics, each about the length of this article, have been issued—"Provisional Guidelines for Local Chapters"; "Retreats for Married Couples—Provisional Guidelines"; "The Case for Marriage Enrichment"; "ACME and the Professionals." Copies may be purchased for $.50 each, including postage. These and other papers are to be published in an ACME Handbook now in preparation.

For further information about ACME, write to 403 South Hawthorne Road, Winston-Salem, N.C. 27103.

MARRIAGE ENCOUNTER

ROBERT J. GENOVESE
Edina, Minnesota

Marriage Encounter is an international movement whose local affiliates offer weekend programs to promote the growth of married couples. As a movement, couples have spread and are spreading the message to other couples that they have found success and happiness in their marriages with the aid of Marriage Encounter. In turn, many of these same couples have become actively involved with the local programs offered by the movement. It is through these weekend programs that Marriage Encounter and the couples within the movement actually share the twin bases of Marriage Encounter—faith and the technique called "dialogue."

HISTORY

To understand the place of Marriage Encounter within the United States, we have to go back to the years shortly after World War II. About 1948, a young couple in Chicago, Pat and Patty Crowley believed that something should be done to foster the enrichment of family life. Because they were Roman Catholic, they began a group which based its discussion techniques on the principles of a Belgian priest, Canon Cardijn. These principles—observe, judge, and act—are oriented toward social action in the immediate community. Within a very short time, other groups got going in the United States and this movement became known as The Christian Family Movement (CFM). CFM became an international organization about 1950.

CFM eventually spread to Spain. But unfortunately, due to the somewhat repressive policies of the Franco government, its social action was attenuated in most cases and nonexistent in others. There was one man in Madrid, Father Gabriel Calvo, who was of the opinion that CFM would soon die unless another focus could be found for the many couples who belonged to the movement within his country.

Father Calvo noticed that several couples in the Madrid CFM seemed to have made a success of their marriages—more so than other couples. He soon contacted a core group of some 28 couples all of whom decided to work with what was possible within their country. Each of these couples had "a profound confidence in each other, unusual love and unity and a deep dialogue with each other." The question was, why not help other couples find these same qualities in their own marriages? So, with the help of these 28 couples, Father Calvo founded *Encuentre Conyugal.*

Marriage Encounter, as it developed in Spain, has four distinct steps. The first is the weekend program for married couples whereby several team couples and a clergyman share their experiences concerning the dimensions of married life as it relates to faith and dialogue. The second step, called a reencounter or *retorno,* centers more on the faith aspect of Marriage Encounter, i.e., how the couples together can better approach God within their own religion, church, or denomination.

The third step is the family encounter, a weekend during which parents and children have a chance to be reconciled in much the same way the couple was in the original encounter. Step four, similar to the intent of step two, involves the whole family reaching out to God after they have been reconciled to one another.

Because the Marriage Encounter was intimately involved with CFM, it began to spread after its beginnings in 1958 to almost every place where CFM was active—except in the United States. Marriage Encounter did not reach this country until 1966, when the first Spanish Encounter was held in Miami for Cuban refugee couples located there.

However, in 1967, Father Calvo along with many of his original couples came to the National CFM Convention that was held at Notre Dame. In one of the workshops they presented their ideas and received a warm reception. One of the couples, Jamie and Arline Whelan of New Jersey encouraged seven other couples to remain at Notre Dame after the convention to make the first American Marriage Encounter. These eight couples were joined by six priests. Because all of the materials were in Spanish, the talks had to be translated by a bilingual couple from Mexico City.

One of the stipulations Father Calvo made before the weekend was to ask those couples and priests who made the weekend to spread Marriage Encounter to the English-speaking world. It was his feeling that Spain was merely repaying its debt of gratitude for the gift of CFM by bringing Marriage Encounter to the United States.

That original group did spread Marriage Encounter. Very soon they translated the Spanish materials into English and were able to present programs in Montreal, Detroit, Chicago, and New Jersey. In 1969 the movement was large enough to have a National Marriage Encounter Board. The Whelans were elected as the first executive couple. Since then, they have been succeeded by Armando and Barbara Carlo along with Father Jake Buettner. These three are the National Executive Team and are officed in Chicago.

One of the peculiarities about Marriage Encounter in this country is that, unlike any other country, it is not a part of CFM. It has its own national and local organizations. Although firm figures are not available, the National Office estimates that between 100,000 and 200,000 couples have participated in weekend programs which have been held in every state since 1967.

As can be seen, Marriage Encounter began in a Catholic country and has had heavy Roman Catholic involvement in this country. But this is accidental—not essential. As the movement spread in our pluralistic society, many have applied its principles in an ecumenical fashion. Hence, the Marriage Encounter movement has been accepted by Jews, those in other Christian churches, and by agnostics, although certain modifications have been made for those groups so as to eliminate that which is peculiarly Roman Catholic. For example, there is a presentation on the weekend titled "The Sacrament of Marriage and Its Graces." Because this is a belief of Roman Catholics almost exclusively, the talk centers more appropriately on the sacredness of the marriage contract for those groups who are not Roman Catholic.

THEORY

The twin bases of Marriage Encounter are faith and dialogue. The former has a theological derivation while the latter has a psychological one.

Even a casual reader of the Bible has to be impressed with the emphasis placed on "word"—whether it be God's creative word or a human word addressed to another human being. From the very first pages of Genesis and on through the remainder of the Jewish Bible and into the Christian Bible, we can see how this concept is portrayed. In fact, without God's word we would not know God. God's word, then, is self-revelatory. Indeed, human words can also share in this quality. They can be self-revelatory of the person uttering them.

The real problem, within our modern world, is that all too often human words do not reveal the person. Instead, they function as "masks," which wall off a person from true human interaction with others. There are very obvious reasons for this. Because we are the inheritors of Graeco-Roman traditions with their emphasis on concepts rather than feelings, we tend to subordinate our feelings in favor of the factual and informational. But, the truly human is bound up intimately with our feelings and so the "factual and informational" words hide and mask off our truly human nature. This is not the case within the Judaeo-Christian tradition, as is evident to anyone who reads the Psalms. They are filled with deep-seated feelings even to the point of what we moderns might term blasphemy. But, that would be to reread the Bible as a Greek—not a Jew.

Theologically, then, Marriage Encounter stresses the very human aspect of feelings, though not to the neglect of the conceptual and informational. It seeks, rather, to regain the balance that must exist between the two.

This notion of "word" is the foundation of Marriage Encounter because Marriage Encounter seeks to revitalize a couple's words within the community of marriage. It tries to get couples to cut through the dullness of routine, the trivia of ordinary living, and the pace of society—all of which rob our words of their strength.

The word that couples speak takes on depth and understanding through the technique of dialogue. First, one spouse personally reflects on himself or herself—taking time to know and understand who he or she really is—all of which is the first and most essential element of love. Then, all of this is written down. This written message to one's spouse makes the individual's words more specific so that the other person can more easily share and understand them. This simple technique deepens the dedication already present in marriage.

A renewal begins. The human word is again full of faith. This renewal is the human foundation that permits the human word to become real in marriage. This personal witness or sharing of one's word is essential to the Marriage Encounter. Without personal sharing, there can never be an intense and deep dialogue between two married people.

THE PROGRAM

To accomplish all this, Marriage Encounter asks a couple to concentrate for 44 hours on their own relationship. They leave behind the children, the job, the home, and all the pressures of daily living. They go apart to another place for a weekend to look at the word they utter to each other to build an even stronger foundation for their marriage.

By sharing their feelings about each other and their life together, they experience a growth in unity. They begin to experience the reality of what the Bible terms, "two in one flesh." By exploring their deepest feelings and emotions, a couple begins to appreciate their own strengths and weaknesses. Because of the love that comes from this sharing, they realize how each is the image of God for each other. They see they have God's Spirit which is love.

The key to this self-revelation is the love, and dedication the couple already have but may only be dimly aware of. The couple, as they move through the weekend, become progressively more aware of the love they have for each other as well as their dependence on the love of God, the foundation and core of their own love.

There are four stages each couple goes through on an Encounter weekend: the "I," the "We," the "We-God," and the "We-God-World" stages.

During the "I" stage the individual comes to understand his or her own personal feelings about himself or herself as a person—the strengths and weaknesses. The honest recognition and sharing that come later depend on this understanding. This stage is based on the principle: "The truth will set you free."

Throughout the "We" stage the individual shares this recognition with his or her spouse. It is a sampling of what it means to love and be loved through all the ups and downs, the routines, and cycles of life. Between any high illusion or low disillusion, there is a balance of peace and love which is the real pattern of life. Understanding the world through the spouse's eyes brings the spirit of "two in one."

In the "We-God" stage, the couple is asked to meditate on God as the Father and Creator of all. His plan, when He made man, was not to leave him alone. Rather, a human being is to love and be loved so that two can image God to each other, their children, and the world around them.

During the final stage, "We-God-World," the couple comes to understand that they cannot remain off by themselves in their love. If they do, their love may end up only as infatuation. So, they come to the realization that their love must flow outward to bring community to the whole family of man.

As can be seen, the total interaction on the weekend takes place between the spouses. So, Marriage Encounter—while it does use the term "encounter"—does not function as a sensitivity group. There is no group interaction during the weekend program. In actuality, the encounter is a rediscovery of self and spouse.

Typically, the Encounter weekends are held at retreat houses. Those making the weekend arrive at about 8 p.m. on Friday. After a short period of time devoted to getting acquainted, the team conducting the weekend will begin the first presentation. Depending on the locale, there are usually ten to twelve talks spread throughout the weekend, with one or more talks devoted to each of the four stages.

During the presentation the team couple (or clergyman) giving the talk merely share their experience on the topic. In no way do these couples or clergymen pose as experts. They are quite clear about this. They are there to serve the couples making the weekend by sharing what they have discovered in themselves and in their own marriages.

After the presentation the individual couples are given time for reflection on certain open-ended questions that relate to the topic just presented. After this period of reflection, the individual spouse writes down his or her reactions to these questions in a notebook provided to each person. Then they share their written reflections with each other in the privacy of their room—or elsewhere of their own choosing. After reading these written reflections, the couple usually pursue their feelings even deeper—but now orally.

Some of the topics of the various presentations by the team couples are as follows: encounter with self, the state of marriage in the modern world, symptoms of spiritual divorce, openness to God's plan, marriage in God's plan, confidence and dialogue, human sexuality, marriage spirituality, and open and apostolic marriage. The flow of the weekend is built around these and similar topics.

We have seen how the couples making the weekend actually do their own "encountering." But what of the team couples that give the weekend? Three couples, along with a clergyman, make up the team who are responsible for the presentations and just about everything else that happens during the weekend, e.g., making sure the meals are served on time, carrying emergency messages to the couples attending, and so on. In addition, they also work at deepening their own relationship through their own continuing dialogue. To prepare themselves for these tasks and responsibilities, each of the team couples and the clergyman must have made a marriage encounter weekend. Second, they must be convinced that Marriage Encounter has done something for them personally—something they want to share with others. And finally, they must be willing to devote themselves to team preparation.

Team preparation can be as simple or as complex as the team wishes to make it. Usually, one or another couple has already given a weekend, although one couple may be a rookie couple. About a month or so before the weekend they are scheduled to give, the whole team meets to select those talks they would be most comfortable giving. Then the couple jointly prepare their talks—usually at home between the first and second meetings. At the second meeting the couples and the clergyman make their presentations to the rest of the team. Then they sit back and listen to the constructive criticism the rest of the team may give about the talk. If more meetings are necessary, these are scheduled. By the time a couple makes their presentation on the weekend, the talk has probably been rewritten several times and delivered a couple of times.

Some areas of the country, e.g., Chicago, provide evenings or days of team enrichment by having speakers address their teams. These speakers are experts in psychology, psychiatry, marriage counseling, and the like. In this way the team can make use of the insights and principles of these social sciences. However, neither the team couples nor the clergyman put themselves in the position of an expert—even if they do have such expertise. The team presents themselves as co-learners and sharers who are equally on the road toward making a successful marriage, just as much as those attending.

RESULTS

The results of this program can only be calculated by the rapidity with which the Marriage Encounter movement is spreading. In New York weekends are booked for as much as two years in advance, even when ten or more retreat houses are being used each weekend. Much the same can be said for other parts of the country. The amazing thing is that the word is spread by the couples who have made the weekend and who want their friends and relatives to gain what they have had during the weekend. There has been some national publicity which, in turn, has brought some enquiries. But, for the most part, it is the enthusiastic response of those who have made the weekend that accounts for the continuing spread of the movement.

A secondary but perhaps very important result is the adaptation of Marriage Encounter to a weekend for those engaged to be married. Called the Engaged Encounter, this weekend began because married couples were convinced that they would have had a far more successful marriage had they learned to dialogue from day one. They decided to share the secret of their success in marriage to benefit those about to be married. One of the areas which has had the most success with this program is Detroit. In the past year, the Engaged Encounter has just about taken the place of every other premarriage preparation program.

But just what does an Encounter weekend mean to the individual couples after they return home? Usually the couple has gone after the wife has overcome the resistance of her husband to attend the weekend. About halfway through, the husband begins to convert to this new style of living and is usually just as enthusiastic as his wife as they renew their marriage vows on Sunday afternoon before they leave. Then the question is: will this couple continue to grow in love for each other?

Experience has shown that those couples who remain committed to an ongoing dialogue (preferably daily) usually remain closely involved with Marriage Encounter. They continue to grow in love for each other and become even more closely "two in one flesh." While the converse is not documented, there is some slight evidence that those couples who give up the practice of dialogue soon find themselves back in the same pattern of life that may have led them to make their Marriage Encounter in the first place.

To assist couples in keeping their commitment, Marriage Encounter has several follow-up programs. For example, the couples who made a weekend together may have a reunion about one month after their weekend. In some areas they hold evenings of renewal about once a month. Elsewhere, couples have formed Image groups or discussion groups (most of which use a manual called *The Encountering Couple*). All these programs try to provide the emotional and community support needed by the individual couple to survive successfully in marriage. In effect, these groups function as an "extended family" for each of the couples who belong to the group.

STRENGTHS AND LIMITATIONS

One of the most obvious strengths of Marriage Encounter is that the movement is helping those marriages and those couples who want to enrich their relationship. These couples have noticed the silver lining has become a bit tarnished—but they believe their love deserves something more. Typically, the couples who make the weekends are a long way from the divorce court and probably have never even thought about seeing a marriage counselor. All they know is that they belong to the 90% to 95% of marriages that really never seem to get away from the usual daily ups and downs. They know it—but they don't like it; and they come to Marriage Encounter to discover a better relationship for themselves. So, in effect, Marriage Encounter can presume the good faith of those who come to its weekends. These couples have something stable on which to build.

But the other side of the coin is that Marriage Encounter has very little follow-up for the couples who come to the weekend as the last resort. They have already been to the marriage counselor and may be thinking of a divorce. Then somebody told them about Marriage Encounter. So they come hoping for a miracle—which usually doesn't happen because the couple has been so out of contact with each other that a single weekend will not repair the damage. These couples need to see professionals; since the team couples are not experts, they need to be referred for outside professional help.

Another limitation or weakness is the fragmentation and internecine conflicts that occur between the various "expressions" of Marriage Encounter in this country. Unfortunately, there is one "expression" which remains Roman Catholic in an almost doctrinaire fashion. In effect, its purpose has become—not the renewal of marriage in society—but the renewal of the Roman Catholic Church through Marriage Encounter. Hence, only Catholics can become leaders within this "expression." Similarly, this group will establish a "counter-expression" even in areas where Marriage Encounter is already quite strong. For these and other reasons, you may be disappointed if you were to recommend that a client make a weekend put on by this "expression,"—or make such a weekend yourself.

In spite of these limitations, the Marriage Encounter movement continues to grow and thrive in the United States. Marriage Encounter is, by no means, the final answer to the manifold problems besetting marriage and the family. But, as of 1974, Marriage Encounter does seem to be one of the more viable means available for couples to begin arriving at their own personal answers to the problems besetting them within their own marriage and family.

NOTE

For further information write the National Marriage Encounter: Barbara and Armando Carlo, 5305 West Foster Ave., Chicago, IL 60630, or phone (312) 736-5505. The address of the monthly magazine for the National Marriage Encounter (*Agape*) is: Jerry and Marilyn Sexton, Minnesota Marriage Encounter, Inc., 897 So. Robert St., St. Paul, MN 55118.

THE MINNESOTA COUPLES COMMUNICATION PROGRAM

ELAM W. NUNNALLY
School of Social Welfare
University of Wisconsin-Milwaukee
SHEROD MILLER
Department of Medicine, Medical School
University of Minnesota
DANIEL B. WACKMAN
School of Journalism and Mass Communication
University of Minnesota

The excerpt following is from a feedback episode in the Minnesota Couples Communication Program—group members are providing feedback to Jim and Carol, one of the participant couples, immediately after a three-minute dialogue between them. In the exercise each couple discusses a real issue for three minutes, and then receives five to ten minutes of feedback from other group members. Feedback focuses on the skills used or missing in their exchange. The exercise occurs toward the end of Session 2, at a point when group members have been introduced to several of the skills and concepts taught in the program. Characteristics of the MCCP illustrated in the excerpt are discussed in the article.

Participant A: "I heard you make a clear 'intention statement,' Jim, when you told Carol that you would like some time for just yourself when you get home from work."

Participant B: "Yeah, he did, and I heard Carol . . ."

Instructor: (interrupting) "Will you speak directly to Carol?"

Participant B: "Okay, Carol, I heard you make a clear 'intention statement' when you told Jim that you want some adult companionship after spending all day with the kids."

Participant C: "I heard some 'checking out' from both; for example, Jim, when you asked Carol whether she thought you were trying to avoid her when you bury your nose in the newspaper, and, Carol, when you asked Jim how he felt about your wanting more of his company in the evening."

Instructor: "Did you note the absence of any skills that you would have liked to hear Carol and Jim use in their dialogue?"

Participant C: "I can't recall either of you saying how you *felt*—no 'feeling statements.' Carol, I was especially aware of this when you were talking about being alone all day with the kids and then Jim comes home and starts reading the paper. I was thinking you might be feeling deprived, or hurt, or angry, or" . . . (another participant, interrupting) . . . "All of the above."

DISTINCTIVE FEATURES OF THE MCCP PROGRAM

SKILLS

The focus is on skills, on process rather than content. This is an educational program in which partners practice using effective communication skills in dialogue around meaningful issues and receive immediate feedback from other participants on skills demonstrated and skills missing from their dialogue. (If one of the group members begins to offer solutions, or begins to speculate about why a couple is having a particular problem, the instructor will interrupt and encourage the participant to limit his feedback to identifying skills used or skills lacking in the dialogue.)

In addition to skill practice in the group session, structure is provided for transfer of learning to situations outside the group through practice assignments to be carried out at home between group sessions. For example, each participant chooses a particular skill to work on in his communication with partner during the following week, and at the beginning of the next session each couple reports back to the group on their progress.

THE DYADIC SYSTEM

In this program the focus is on the dyad rather than on the individual or on relationships among nonpartners in the group. Feedback is addressed to partners about the communication skills and patterns observable in the couple's interaction. This contrasts with an encounter group where the focus may be on a single individual, e.g., how he comes across to one or more of the other participants in the group.

MCCP groups are composed of "live systems." Each partnership has its own past, present, and anticipated future patterns of relating. Each participant learns with his partner within the context of the system for which his learning is intended—the couple. This feature distinguishes MCCP from programs in which partners attend individually in hopes of bringing back something to the relationship. In MCCP they bring their relationship to the program.

Because of its live system characteristic, instructors must have considerable skill in order to effectively lead an MCCP group. The instructor must be able to accept and help partners deal with a range of possibilities which may be experienced within a three-minute dialogue without getting into counseling.

GROUP CONTEXT FOR LEARNING

One advantage of a group context for learning—as distinguished from a context in which a couple meets alone with an instructor—is that the couple has an opportunity to receive feedback from peers, from other couples like themselves who are there to improve communication skills. In a warmly supportive peer group a couple receives encouragement to learn and permission to make mistakes in the process of learning. Another advantage of the group context is that each participant has many opportunities to identify skills used by other participants and to practice giving "useful" feedback. In the feedback episode at the start of the paper, there were several examples of useful feedback: specific skills were identified and descriptive behavioral data reported so that the recipients could know just what the observer saw and heard that led him to identify a particular skill. When a participant offers merely an impression (e.g., "I heard a putdown."), the instructor will ask the participant to report *what* he heard or saw, i.e., what was the impression based upon: "What did you hear Jim say that sounded to you like . . . " and so on. The many opportunities provided in the group context for giving and for receiving quality feedback serve to heighten participants' awareness of interaction patterns and to integrate skills necessary for successful relationship work.

VOLUNTARISM

Another characteristic of MCCP is conveyed by the terms voluntarism and participant choice. We assume that learning is most effective when the learning experience is voluntary, that is, when an individual takes initiative for his own learning. Before joining a group each couple meets with an instructor to discover what the program is designed to teach and to clarify whether or not this is what each partner is seeking. If they elect to join the program, the "contract" is for active, conjoint participation of both partners. During the group sessions participation remains voluntary: at any point during a group session, one or both members of a couple may choose to participate or not in a particular exercise, or to receive group feedback on their interaction process. Each couple privately reaches a conjoint decision about what they are willing to discuss, prior to initiating a couple-dialogue for the group to observe and provide feedback.

OBJECTIVES AND RATIONALE

The immediate objectives of the MCCP program are to equip partners with (1) tools for heightening self-awareness, other-awareness and interactional awareness, and (2) communication skills for creating more effective and mutually satisfying interaction patterns, if they choose to do so. The longer-run objectives are to increase the flexibility of the dyadic system in dealing with change and to enhance the autonomous functioning of the partners. With heightened awareness and with skills to express that awareness, graduates of the program can choose to play, to debate, to speculate and openly disclose themselves, utilizing modes of communication appropriate to their intentions at the moment. The program is aimed at equipping partners to become active agents in building their relationship, rather than mere responders to events that "happen" to them.

The emphasis on acquiring skills and concepts for building or remaking an intimate relationship results from our conception of couple relationships as ever-changing systems, influenced both by events occurring outside the system (changes of job, residence, financial and social opportunities) and by changes occurring within the system (aging, addition of a new member, changes in value priorities). Our view of the couple relationship as a dynamic, developmental process is reflected in a model of organizational development (see Figure 1).

Looking at the phases presented in the model, we view disruption as a fact of life, an ever-recurring phenomenon in intimate relationships. If a couple lacks skills for renegotiating, the partners will usually try to return to the way things used to be. They probably cannot return to the status quo because the disruption introduces new contingencies and new awareness into the system, which, for better or worse, differentiates the system-in-the-present from the system-as-it-was-before. Failing to return to "the way things used to be," some couples resign themselves to a depleted relationship at

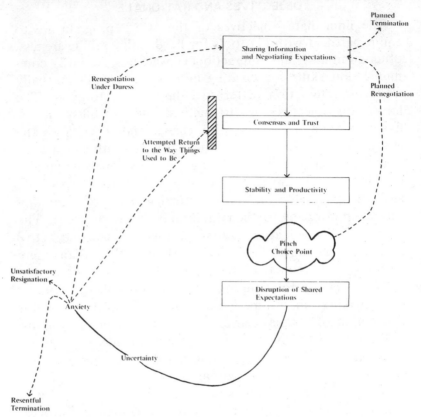

SOURCE: Sherwood and Scherer, 1975; adapted by the authors for this paper.

Figure 1: PREVENTIVE MAINTENANCE MODEL FOR COUPLES

the expense of personal growth and mutual relational satisfactions, a status which one family sociologist has termed "holy deadlock" (LeMasters, 1959). Another option is to terminate the relationship, an option chosen by an increasing proportion of married couples, usually after some years of alternating between resignation and unsuccessful attempts to create change.

Couples equipped with skills for monitoring interaction patterns and effectively expressing their awareness are better able to move into a new phase of sharing information and negotiating expectations, reestablishing consensus and trust. Furthermore, these couples more often are able to head off a major disruption by initiating planned renegotiation when a "pinch" is first noted. Examples of "pinch" messages follow:

I'm getting to feel more and more envious of all your outside interests, and more and more frustrated about not being able to do something with my college education. I want to do something about it. You up to talking about it now?

I thought your going to work was a good idea, and I guess I still think so in a way; but, I'm feeling over-loaded with doing my share of the housework in addition to the extra hours I'm having to put in at the office. I'd like to figure out some way to deal with this.

When a couple lacks ability to identify a "pinch," the partners may enter a period of acting out negative feelings— escalating toward a disruptin—instead of disclosing their impressions, feelings, and intentions directly and dealing with the issue explicitly. A relatively simple personal issue (e.g., one partner feeling overloaded with work) is less likely to evolve into a complex relationship issue (e.g., who counts most or who decides) when the partners are able to tune in to feelings and wants, disclose these directly, identify the issue involved, and openly discuss alternative solutions.

ORIGINS AND THEORETICAL BASES

Work on the program was initiated in 1968 by a small group of researchers, theorists, and therapists from the University of Minnesota Family Study Center and the Family and Children's Agency of Minneapolis. The project group was influenced by family development theorists (e.g., Hill and Rodgers, 1964: 171-211; Rapaport, 1963), symbolic interactionists (e.g., Foote and Cottrell, 1955; Foote, 1963; Turner, 1962), and modern systems and communication theory, particularly as presented by theorists working in the areas of marriage, family, and group therapy (e.g., Watzlawick et al.,

1967; Satir, 1967; Hill, 1965, 1967; Bateson, 1942; Ruesch and Bateson, 1951).

The family development literature suggested that couples and families move through recognizable stages in their careers together, and that critical role transitions occur as they move from one stage to another, i.e., successful handling of certain developmental tasks facilitates satisfactory transition.

The study team focused on identifying skills and developing skill training modalities in order to equip couples to meet the challenge of their developmental tasks, accommodate to change, and even to create change in order to keep the relationship viable over time. Assuming effective communication to be basic to developmental processes, the team turned to systems and communication theory. The literature suggested that the social system which functions most effectively has rules which both define interaction patterns to insure some degree of stability, and at the same time, provide procedures for changing patterns to maintain flexibility and to deal with conflict (Speer, 1970; Sprey, 1966). Thus, to provide for both stability and for change within the system, the team designed a program around two sets of skills: (1) skills to enable partners to understand their rules and interaction patterns, i.e., awareness skills, and (2) skills to enable them to change their rules and interaction patterns, i.e., communication skills.

MCCP SKILLS AND CONCEPTUAL FRAMEWORKS

In the first session participants are introduced to "the awareness wheel," a framework for identifying dimensions of self-awareness to help them tune into their own self-information. They also learn specific skills for verbally expressing their awareness, congruently and self-responsibly. For example:

> I'd like to go out more often with you. (self-responsible—speaking for self)

NOT

You never want to go anywhere! (overresponsible—speaking for other)

OR

It would be nice to go out. (underresponsible—speaking for no one)

In the second session the focus shifts to listening skills, skills for facilitating partner's self-disclosure, skills for assuring that each partner's messages are understood accurately. Three specific behavioral skills are introduced, along with the "shared meaning" conceptual framework for matching messages sent with messages received.

The third session is built around the "communication styles framework" which can be used effectively to "step outside" the system and talk about "what's happening." This is a form of verbal metacommunication essential to the process of "planned renegotiation." In the process of identifying the differential impact and utilities of alternative communication styles, couples become more aware of their choices: what they communicate and how they communicate.

In the fourth session, attention centers on the relation between skills and styles and one's intention to build or to diminish self- and other-esteem. One additional framework is presented to help integrate all material presented in the program and to facilitate the creation of patterns for effective work on relationship issues.

PROGRAM FORMAT

Groups are composed of five to seven couples who meet with one or two certified MCCP instructors for twelve hours, usually in three-hour sessions meeting weekly for four weeks. Some instructors like to schedule the first three sessions in a weekend retreat, with the fourth session following a week to ten days later. Each session builds upon lecturettes, exercises, feedback, and discussions from prior sessions. The book, *Alive and Aware: Improving Communication in Relationships,* supplements the work carried on in the group sessions and provides a number of exercises to help couples practice at home, thereby transfering learning to their everyday relationship outside the group.[1]

MCCP INSTRUCTORS AND INSTRUCTOR TRAINING

While instructors do not have to be married, or even teach the program with a partner, many MCCP instructors prefer to co-lead couples' groups with their spouse. Leading groups as a couple increases credibility when participants see the instructor-couple utilizing the frameworks and skills themselves. Working jointly can provide fun and work; it can also provide opportunities for both partners to join together in helping others to grow.

In MCCP the instructor reduces his own social and psychological distance from the group by doing any of the things he asks participants to do. The instructor differs from participants primarily by the number and quality of the roles he is competent and prepared to carry out. As a member the instructor demonstrates his involvement by receiving as well as giving feedback. In doing this, he dispels doubts participants may have had about his own personal commitment to growth and development. As a teacher the instructor tries creatively to include participants in understanding and mastering the materials presented. He articulates and demonstrates the goals, frameworks, and specific behavioral skills of the program. The instructor who has personally integrated the conceptual frameworks and the communication skills into his own life senses that he has something to teach and that he is prepared to do so. He shows his own convictions about the usefulness of what he has to teach through his own personal familiarity, comfort, and competence with the material he is teaching.

MCCP instructors represent a number of professional disciplines including social work, clinical psychology, psychiatry, education, and the ministry. The prerequisite, however, for enrolling in an instructor training workshop is not a professional degree but rather experience and ability in group leadership. The first step toward certification is the completion of a three-day instructor training workshop.[2] Following the training workshop, the instructor-trainee conducts three MCCP couples' intern groups and secures written evaluations from group participants. Participant evaluations provide an important additional basis for approval or for denial of certification. Instructor-trainees and instructors are invited and encouraged to attend periodically scheduled review workshops.

Interpersonal Communication Programs, Inc. does not enter into any franchise arrangements with instructors; hence, instructors are free to serve whom they wish, and they are also free to determine what fee will be charged to couples enrolling in an MCCP course. ICP, Inc. has certain expectations for instructors, but these expectations have to do only with professional competence and responsibility.

EVALUATION OF THE PROGRAM.

Effects of the MCCP were tested in a field experiment. Descriptions of the experiment and the findings are available (Miller, 1971; Nunnally, 1971: Miller, Nunnally, and Wackman, 1974). In brief, the findings indicated that the MCCP increases participants' awareness of dyadic interaction and leads to greater use of communication styles appropriate to work on relationship issues. The field experiment was not designed to assess the long-range impact of communication training on the couples' relationships, and research directed to this issue is needed.

At the present time assessment of the impact of MCCP on couples' relationships is obtained informally through reports from instructors and from several hundred participants. (Approximately 800 MCCP groups have been conducted.) Typical of the positive comments offered by participants are the following.

> A very effective way of bringing out one's awareness and how to use this awareness in everyday situations. We have leaned it is possible to disagree without an all-out fight. The skills can be applied with anyone if I try, and I have had some success with the children, too.

> This experience has really done wonders for me. I was always taught not to show feelings. I have now been able to break that barrier and discuss real feelings without fear of being put down.

> We have learned we don't have to be defensive with each other.

> More awareness of myself as a separate person, different from my partner. More courage to share this difference. More confidence in myself.

> Very, Very positive changes in our couple relationship and also carry-over to my relations with others. "Intention statements" were difficult for me, and since the course I can feel comfortable with it.

> Prior to the program I valued open communication but lacked skills. The program presented me with a framework from which to operate. We now have a "shared meaning" of what desirable communication is.

> We are much more secure with each other now that we have a way to work out everyday problems.

> Frankly, I have been amazed that such "simple concepts" have been able to help our relationship so much.

Relatively few negative reactions to the program have been observed. Such criticism as has been received usually falls along one of the following lines: (1) concern that gains made during the program will not be maintained after the program ends, (2) belief that the program is too short (twelve hours) to permit integration of the material, (3) disappointment that the spouse did not learn as much as the participant had hoped. Consistent with the low rate of negative criticisms, "dropping out" appears to be a rare phenomenon. We believe that the practice of holding a ten- to fifteen-minute presession interview with each couple—to assess the commitment of each partner to the objectives of the program—is an important factor in the couples' satisfaction with the program and low frequency of drop-outs. In response to criticisms 1 and 2 above, many instructors now regularly plan for one or more sessions following the termination of the twelve-hour series. Instructors report that these follow-up sessions appear to be very useful in helping couples to continue utilizing skills learned in the program.

At the present time MCCP has proven attractive primarily to people with at least some college education. Some modifications may be required to make the program attractive to less educated couples. A limitation on the program is the necessity to restrict size of the training group to not more than seven couples. The size limitation results in a cost to participants higher than would be the case if the group could include ten or twelve couples. The size limitation is necessary when working with "live systems" so that enough time and attention can be given to each couple to avoid incomplete training experiences, i.e., heightening awareness without skill or choice.

Experience with more than 800 groups has revealed several advantages of the program.

(1) The program has been found to be beneficial to partners at any point in their career (pairing, living together, during marriage, or in anticipation of remarriage).

(2) Groups have been conducted in a number of different settings—churches, university continuing-education divisions, YMCAs, social agencies, and the like.

(3) Although the program is clearly educational and developmental rather than therapeutic in objectives and structure, marriage and family counselors report that the program can be an extremely valuable complement to counseling and therapy. (In no way, however, does this imply that the program can or should be viewed as a substitute for counseling or therapy. In using the

program as a complement to therapy, the therapist will need to give consideration to group composition and to the timing of the MCCP experience in relation to the stages of therapy.)

(4) The program offers a meaningful supplement, or alternative, to more traditional methods of preparation for marriage.

(5) Finally, the program can be offered as a module within a "functional" college or university course in marriage, family, or interpersonal relations.

SUMMARY

The Minnesota Couples Communication Program offers a structured educational experience directed toward equipping couples with skills for (1) heightening awareness of self and self's contributions to interaction, (2) effectively expressing this self-awareness, (3) accurately understanding partner's communications, and (4) flexibly choosing to maintain or to change ways of relating to one another. The program is conducted by instructors who are certified after completion of an instructor training workshop and receipt of favorable evaluations by participant couples.

NOTES

1. This book is available from the publisher: Interpersonal Communication Programs, Inc., 2001 Riverside Avenue, Minneapolis, Minnesota, 55454 ($7.95).

2. Instructor training workshops are conducted in many localities in the United States and Canada. Information about dates, locations, costs, and other details can be obtained by writing to Interpersonal Communication Programs, Inc., 2001 Riverside Avenue, Minneapolis, Minnesota, 55454.

REFERENCES

BATESON, G. (1942) "Social planning and the concept of Deutero-Learning." Science, Philosophy and Religion, Second Symposium 2: 81-97.

FOOTE, N. N. (1963) "Matching of husband and wife in phases of development," pp. 15-21 in M. B. Sussman (ed.) Sourcebook in Marriage and the Family. Boston: Houghton Mifflin.

——— and L. S. Cottrell, Jr. (1955) Identity and Interpersonal Competence: A New Direction in Family Research. Chicago: Univ. of Chicago Press.

HILL, R. and R. RODGERS (1964) "The developmental approach," chapter 5 in H. T. Christensen (ed.) Handbook on Marriage and the Family. Chicago: Rand McNally.

HILL, W. F. (1967) A Guide to Understanding the Structure and Function of the Hill Interaction Matrix. Los Angeles: University of Southern California Youth Studies Center.

——— (1965) Hill Interaction Matrix: A Method of Studying Interaction in Psychotherapy Groups. Los Angeles: University of Southern California Youth Studies Center.

LeMASTERS, E. E. (1959) "Holy deadlock: a study of unsuccessful marriages." Soc. Q. 21: 86-91.

MILLER, S. (1971) "The effects of communication training in small groups upon self-disclosure and openness in engaged couples' systems of interaction: a field experiment." Ph.D. dissertation. University of Minnesota.

MILLER, S., E. NUNNALLY, and D. WACKMAN (forthcoming) "A communication training program for couples." (submitted for publication, 1974)

——— (1974) Alive and Aware: Improving Communication in Relationships. Minneapolis: Interpersonal Communication Programs, Inc.

NUNNALLY, E. W. (1971) "Effects of communication training upon interaction awareness and empathic accuracy of engaged couples: a field experiment." Ph.D. dissertation. University of Minnesota.

RAPOPORT, R. (1963) "Normal crisis, family structure and mental health." Family Process 2 (March): 3-11.

RUESCH, J. and G. BATESON (1951) Communication: The Social Matrix of Psychiatry. New York: W. W. Norton.

SHERWOOD, J. J. and J. J. SCHERER (1975) "A model for couples: how two can grow together." Small Group Behavior 6, 1 (February): 11-29.

SPEER, D. C. (1970) "Family systems: morphostasis and morphogenesis or 'is homeostasis enough?' " Family Process 9, 3: 259-278.

SPREY, J. (1966) "The family as a system in conflict." J. of Marriage and the Family 31 (November): 699-706.

TURNER, R. H. (1962) "Role taking: process versus conformity," in A. M. Rose (ed.) Human Behavior and Social Processes. Boston: Houghton Mifflin.

WATZLAWICK, P., J. H. BEAVIN, and D. D. JACKSON (1967) Pragmatics of Human Communication: A Study of Interaction Patterns, Pathologies and Paradoxes. New York: W. W. Norton.

COMMUNICATION TRAINING IN THE SECOND CHANCE FAMILY

DANIEL I. MALAMUD
School of Continuing Education
New York University

For many years I have been involved in designing an adult education course focused on learning about one's self in personally meaningful ways. My interest in such a course grew as I came to realize that there are too few therapists to meet the needs of all who seek therapy, let alone a much larger population of "normals" who need to learn new ways of relating to themselves and others as a means of living more fully. Many who need therapy are either unaware of their need or shrink from it but might be receptive to attending a class, and there are great numbers of "normals" who might profit to a significant degree from a level of experiential education which was not as intensive or extended an experience as is involved in psychotherapy.

Spurred by these convictions, I began leading a "Workshop in Self-Understanding" at New York University's School of Continuing Education in 1950. At first I used films as "real life" stimuli for students to react to in their own personal ways. Their reactions then became the subject matter to be explored and understood. Gradually I dropped films in favor of exercises which were brief and simple, yet stimulated the participants to observe themselves in action and to consider the personal significance of their behavior. These early versions of the course are described in session-by-session detail elsewhere (Malamud, 1955, 1958, 1960, 1965, 1969). Currently I am organizing the workshop around the formation and training of "second chance families," small groups that members create from among themselves with the aim of providing each participant with a "support system" for self-exploration, and which may continue to meet on their own after the course is over (Malamud, 1971, 1972, 1973, 1974). This paper outlines the present status of the workshop with particular emphasis on describing several training exercises that exemplify how I attempt to stimulate members to recognize their habitual patterns of communication and/or to try out new ways that may be more effective. In offering this abbreviated report I hope to convey the nature of the workshop approach sufficiently to stimulate others to try out some of its procedures in new contexts and with different populations.

SUMMARY COURSE DESCRIPTION

My orientation as a group leader has been affected by many influences including my psychoanalytic training at the William Alanson White Institute, Rogers' (1961) views on self-directed learning, Assagioli's (1965) system of psycho-synthesis, and my first-hand experiences with Perls (1969). Perhaps most important have been my encounters with specific students who brought me up short and made me reexamine assumptions I had taken for granted. I am especially grateful to those members who first inspired the concept of the second chance family when they told me how much closer they felt to other members of the class than to their own families.

The workshop is now entitled, "Self-Exploration Through the Second Chance Family." Its course description in the New York University bulletin opens as follows: "This Workshop explores the creative possibilities of a new kind of family, based on personal ties of peers who relate to each other because of a common belief in personal growth. Workshop participants create from among themselves Second Chance Families that aim to provide new opportunities for personal development that members may not have had in their actual childhood families. These families work toward developing a group spirit in which each member feels free to examine himself with minimum defensiveness, learns to give and take both nourishment and challenge, and tries out new ways of behaving."

The course is noncredit and consists of fourteen sessions meeting once a week for close to two hours. In addition to sessions in the classroom families meet without me once a week at times and places of their own choosing. It is understood that families that "click" can continue meeting on their own after the course ends. Members who wish to can repeat the course as often as they like.

The workshop is open to the adult public at large. The 25 to 30 adults who register for the course each term are heterogeneous in age and educational background. There are usually more women than men, and most members come from a middle-class background. In one typical class, members included a Chinese girl who was brought up to value self-containment, a recently divorced woman who was seeking "a different road" for herself, a worker with teenage drug addicts who was interested in learning new group techniques, and a withdrawn young woman referred by her therapist in order to have a preparatory group experience prior to entering his therapy group.

In the opening sessions members become acquainted with each other through a series of structured interactions which provide opportunities for every member to interact with every other member in a variety of ways. Also, in each of the early sessions I break up the group on a random basis into tentative families which meet after class to engage in exercises which I assign. The composition of these families shifts from one session to the next until final families are formed.

After the get-acquainted period, participants practice the formation of families through repeated dry runs. Each time a practice family is formed, members explore what feelings were stirred up in the process, how satisfied or dissatisfied they feel being together, and what they might like to do differently in the next dry run. Families disband as soon as these themes have been discussed, and new groupings are formed. Through such preparatory experiences the participant begins to examine his motives for wanting or not wanting to be with different people, his style of inviting or waiting to be invited, and his reactions to rejecting others or to being rejected himself.

Some time during the middle of the course families are formed "for real." The overall format for forming final families consists of a series of rounds and time-outs. A round is a fifteen-minute period during which members engage in the work of forming families. The time-out is a five-minute break during which members meet in prearranged trios to explore their reactions to the just completed round and to give each other whatever support and advice seems appropriate for the next round. The class agrees in advance on the number of families to be formed and how many members are to be in each (usually a total of eight to ten). Families then form step by step around nuclear pairs. A detailed description of the family formation process may be found elsewhere (Malamud, 1974).

Once the final families are formed I introduce communication training exercises designed to enable them to work productively on their own. Examples of such training experiences will be presented later in this paper.

In the last phase of the course I introduce self-confrontation experiences. These are structured activities which involve time limits, rules, and planned sequences of events; embrace elements of meditation, fantasy, and/or action; elicit a wide variety of responses (often those that would not ordinarily occur spontaneously); and are followed by family discussions. Below is a summary of "seeds," one such structured experience.

I tell members: "In this exercise your family will plant a good seed in you. This seed will be a single sentence addressed to yourself, composed by you, and coming to grips with some special issue in your life, a sentence reflecting a basic attitude or conviction which would mean a great deal to you were it really to take root in the very center of your being. For example, 'Ruth, you don't have to live up to your mother's expectations.' "

The planting takes place in several steps. First, the member shares with his family the seed sentence he wishes to have planted in him and says something briefly about its personal significance. He then steps into the center of the family circle, closes his eyes, and listens receptively as the family chants his seed sentence repeatedly in unison until he raises his hand as a signal for them to stop. Next, one family member at a time comes up to him, addresses his seed sentence to him with conviction and touches him in some way that conveys the member's deep desire to plant the person's seed. Once planting is completed, the person in the center returns to his seat, and another member shares his seed for planting.

My style is geared toward catalyzing a gradual accumulation of special moments in which the participant, moving at his own pace, gets in deeper-than-usual touch with his privately experienced self and/or his self-in-encounter. I do not believe in pressing for "instant intimacy" or pushing for dramatic breakthroughs. Nevertheless, it is inevitable that students develop anxiety at one point or another: the course's subject matter is the student himself; the methods used are provocative and emotionally involving; defenses are challenged. In order to avoid an excess of anxiety with its accompanying confusion and flight, the following safeguards have become a built-in part of the course. I communicate in my comments and especially in my behavior my view of human beings as complex, more alike than otherwise, and inevitably fallible. I stress the desirability of seeing one's mistakes, problems, and shortcomings as inevitable outcomes of life experiences rather than simply as faults deserving self-condemnation. To reinforce this perspective I assign such books as *Guide to Rational Living* (Ellis and Harper, 1961) and *I'm OK—You're OK* (Harris, 1969) to be read and discussed in family meetings.

The introduction of experiences are timed to fit the apparent readiness of the group. I make it a practice to participate in these experiences frequently and to share my personal responses as openly as I can, thus setting an example for the rest of the group. I make it clear that I value privacy highly, and that no student is under compulsion to share more of himself than he wishes. Indeed he has full freedom in deciding how far, if at all, he wishes to become involved in any exercise. The first or last ten minutes of each session are set aside for the airing of any unexpressed disturbances or negative feelings. I encourage members to share in their family meetings unfinished business and unresolved tensions that may be carried over from the classroom experience. Periodically, I invite students to write brief letters to me, and these help me to maintain a supportive, personal bond with each participant.

COMMUNICATION TRAINING

In my first conception of the second chance family I saw it as a medium which, once formed, would facilitate its members' self-exploration. I soon realized, however, that most students lack in varying degrees some of the most elementary skills in how to communicate effectively. For example, they need to learn how to air thoughts and feelings in a self-searching way, listen with minimal interfering static, respond supportively to another's expressions of feelings, give and take feedback, and participate in meetings in ways that make for productive group movement. Finding and developing ways of meeting these needs became a necessity if I were to fulfill my conception of the family as a unit that could become increasingly autonomous and self-directed. Therefore, I have been centering my current interest on developing a number of training exercises that aim at stimulating members to recognize and evaluate their habitual communication patterns and/or practice new and potentially more useful ways of interacting. Following are detailed descriptions of some of these exercises.

SHARE AND LISTEN[1]

I instruct the class as follows: "In this experience you will explore what it is like to be listened to deeply by another person and to listen deeply yourself as this person in turn shares with you. The general format is this: The group breaks up into pairs. Each pair decides who is A and who is B. Member A shares his thoughts and feelings around a particular theme for five minutes while B listens. Then B shares his thoughts and feelings about a selected theme for five minutes while A listens. When each partner has shared with the other, form new pairings with other members and repeat the sharing-listening process. Then, again new pairings, etc., until I call time. Explore a different theme with each new partner. Pairs need not choose the same theme. Select themes from the following list:

— My patterns of listening to others

— My willingness to discuss my personal feelings with others

— My awareness of others' feelings and motivations

— How my way of talking affects others

— Dealing with hurt and angry feelings in myself and others

— My reactions to giving and receiving criticism

— My willingness to trust others

— My reactions to affection and appreciation from others

— My ability to influence others

— My concern about others' reactions

"When you are sharing your thoughts and feelings on a theme, remember that you need not talk continuously. It's OK to pause from time to time to see what you feel like saying next. If you run out of things to say, feel free to close your eyes and wait passively for some new feeling, thought, or sensation to rise to the surface of consciousness. What you say need not be organized, logically connected, or even clearly articulated. Allow yourself to grope for those feelings, thoughts, and associations which you have never before put into words. Each theme can be explored from a number of different perspectives. For example, you might relate the theme to your current experiences in or out of class, or you might recall pertinent incidents from childhood, or you might even allow yourself to fantasy or create a daydream about some aspect of the topic. Be sure to keep in touch with your feelings as you talk or remain silent, and be open to airing how they change.

"Use your turn to share as an opportunity to explore your theme in greater depth than you ordinarily might on your own. See if under the special conditions of this exercise you can arrive at some new perspective, realization, or thought-provoking question about yourself, or can get in touch with hitherto below the surface feelings. Remember, your chances of experiencing something meaningful, even within five minutes, increase to the extent that (a) you do not pressure yourself to achieve or perform well, and (b) you are able to experience your partner as a sincerely receptive listener.

"Do not say anything when it's your turn to be a listener. Be aware of your urges to question, agree or disagree, advise, pass judgment, etc., but remain absolutely silent. Just listen! But not in your ordinary way. Your listening should be extraordinary—alert, attentive, and interested. Convey an attitude which will put your partner so much at ease that he will feel unusually free to explore various aspects of his theme with increasing depth and emotional involvement. By means of facial expression, eye contact, smiles, posture, and gesture convey to your partner such sentiments as the following: I am with you. I want very much to learn about you, what your world is like, and how you see and experience things in it. I accept you as you are. You are entitled to your feelings and your ways of seeing things. I do not wish to change you. Whatever you choose to share with me I wish to hear and to understand as deeply as I can, and I accept it as a precious gift. Rest assured that whatever your difficulties, shortcomings, or hangups, I accept you as a fallible human being, like the rest of us, who has the capacity and the right to grow and develop in your own way and at your own pace.

"Avoid mechanical nods and smiles, poker-faced expressions, and critical grimaces. Don't look around to see what other pairs are doing. Be as natural and as relaxed as you can be. You need not convert this exercise into a grim, life and death test of your skill as a listener.

"If your sharing partner lapses into silence, convey your relaxed acceptance of such silence. It's OK to give him a hand squeeze, pat on the shoulder, or some other touch that conveys empathic support if it feels natural to you, occurs at an appropriate time, and if you sense your partner will not be uneasy by your gesture.

"Some final instructions: When you and your partner have both had turns at sharing and listening, say good-bye in some nonverbal way, a handshake or hug, or whatever feels appropriate, but no words, please. If you find yourself without a partner, simply listen in on any pair, but ask permission first. Be as aware as you can be in each pairing experience, of those factors which interfere with your sharing and listening and those which you find facilitating."

RESOLVING INTERPERSONAL TENSIONS

I introduce this exercise with a brief statement along the following lines: "Tensions develop from time to time in any relationship, even between the closest of friends. In this exercise we will have an opportunity to study tensions which exist among ourselves in this group (including me), explore some of their underlying dynamics, and take some steps toward resolving them as constructively as possible. Toward these ends we will form families within which we will try to work out our tensions as constructively as possible.

"There are many sources of interpersonal tension. As I review my own life I can recall feeling tense in such instances as the following: I wanted a colleague's approval so much that I was shy and tongue-tied in his presence. I felt 'crowded' by a woman who wanted to be closer to me than I did to her. Someone neglected to invite me to join a group, and I reacted with hurt. I found myself dismayingly competitive with a boasting colleague and had an urge to deflate him. A student who behaved in an overly flattering way toward me stirred my distrust, while a silent student who frequently had a contemptuous look on his face aroused anxious feelings in me.

"None of these tensions necessarily reflected a dislike for the person himself, although I have, of course, experienced such global aversions frequently enough, sometimes, I must admit, based on no more than the person's looks reminding me of some disliked person from my past.

"Now consider each of the members in our group (remembering to include me) and select a few of us in relation to whom you are currently experiencing some kind of discomfort, frustration, hurt, or irritation, however slight, that you would like to air, clarify, and possibly resolve. For example, there may be someone in the group that you have been avoiding, out of fear or some other feeling, or you might like the person, but he has certain traits that rub you the wrong way, or you may have had some experience with this person, one that you never discussed with him and that left you with a bad taste in your mouth."

Tension-resolving families are then formed in several ways. For example, I ask, "Who has a tension he would like to work through with somebody else?" Member A says he has a bone to pick with member B, and B agrees to form a pair with him. Two other pairs are formed in a similar manner. Each pair-member then chooses a feedback-observer, and the pairs become quartets. Remaining members then elect to join one or another of the three quartets. I see to it that there are an approximately equal number in each final group.

Once tension families are formed they locate themselves in separate areas of the classroom. A and B, the nuclear pair of a family, sit facing each other and interact in a sequence of four structures with the aim of clarifying and resolving the tension in question. The other members of the group surround A and B and pay close attention to their inter-actions so that they can at designated points share observa-tions and reactions which may be useful.

The first structure consists of two rounds. In the first round member A (who originally asked B to form a pair with him) initiates a "three-step dialogue" with B. This mini-dialogue consists of an opening statement by A, B's response, and A's closing reaction to B's statement. In A's opening statement he briefly tells B what the nature of his tension with B is. Member B responds with an expression of his immediate feeling reaction to A's opening statement and then adds whatever response seems appropriate to the content of A's statement. Member A then makes a closing response which includes his immediate feeling reactions. At the completion of this first dialogue, A and B receive feedback from each of the other members. A and B listen silently throughout the feedback without getting into any discussions with each other or with the other members.

The above procedure is repeated in the next round, except that it is B who now initiates the three-step dialogue. At the conclusion of this first structure A and B check out with each other whether any tensions remain. If not, they become feedback-observers, and two other members of the family with a tension between them engage in the series of structures. On the other hand, if tension remains between A and B, they begin the second structure.

The second structure consists of three one-minute rounds with group feedback given after each round. In the first round A and B converse with each other; the existing tension is the focus. Either one may begin this dialogue. One of the observers calls time at the end of a minute. A and B then listen silently to the group's feedback. In the second round A and B set their chairs aside, stand and face each other, and interact nonverbally without any talking whatsoever until one-minute time is called. In the final round they again engage in free verbal exchange.

If after the above experience their tension continues unresolved, A and B enter the third structure. Member A faces an empty chair placed opposite him and imagines that B is sitting it it. He then initiates a three-step dialogue addressing his image of B. A then sits in B's chair, and role-playing B, responds to A's opening statement. In role-playing B, A attempts to become B as deeply as he can and tries to see the interpersonal situation as sympathetically as he can from B's point of view. After role-playing B's response, A returns to his original chair and makes a closing statement in response to what "B" just said. During this dialogue the other members of the group, including B, are silent observers, listening very closely but not interrupting A in any way.

Member B now engages in a three-step dialogue with his image of A. B faces an empty chair in which he imagines A is seated. In his opening statement to "A" he picks up where the real member A left off and responds to A's closing statement. Then he sits in A's chair and role-plays A's response as sympathetically as he can from A's point of view. Finally, he returns to his chair, becomes himself again, and makes a closing statement in response to what "A" stated. Again the group listens deeply and silently.

After B completes his three-step dialogue with his image of A each member of the group gives feedback to A and B, sharing observations, personal feeling reactions, and whatever suggestions might be facilitating. Throughout this feedback A and B listen deeply but silently. After this feedback, if tensions remain between A and B, they move into the last structure.

In the final structure A and B dialogue freely for five minutes following the Rogerian (1961) rule: "Before making a statement of your own, show that you have been listening by restating what was just expressed to the speaker's satisfaction." During the interaction the observers listen silently except when they find it necessary to remind A or B of the rule. Once time is called, A and B again listen silently to the family's feedback. When feedback is complete, A and B each make closing statements to the group (not to each other!). These closing statements may include reports on the degree to which the original tension has been resolved, reactions to the feedback, new insights, and so on. The group listens silently to these closing statements without any interruptions. Once both closing statements have been made the encounter between A and B is considered at an end whether their tensions have been resolved or not, and the group moves on to repeat this overall format with a new pair.

FAMILY MINI-MEETING

I tell the class: "In this exercise you will have an opportunity to study and assess your spontaneous ways of relating to each other in a family meeting and to explore what new ways of participating you might choose to practice in future meetings. More specifically, I will break you up into a number of families. Each family will obtain a numerical rating for its sense of well-being as a group, and then engage in a thirty-minute meeting with the aim of improving this rating.

"First, let me introduce you to the Emotion Meter. The Meter is a fantasy instrument which can measure the magnitude of any particular feeling or attitude that we may want to focus on. Close your eyes and visualize how your Meter looks. Some of you may see it as a kind of thermometer; for others it may resemble a weighing scale or a mileage gauge. Whatever its appearance, you will notice that the Meter has gradations from zero to 100 and includes an indicator arrow which rests at zero. One hundred stands for the highest magnitude of a particular emotion or attitude under study, and zero, the lowest. For your first measurement, focus on the degree to which you are experiencing a sense of well-being, that is, how generally satisfied and contented you are feeling with yourself right now. To activate the Meter, place your right hand over your heart. Notice that the arrow begins to oscillate between 0 and 100. Within thirty seconds it will come to rest at a point on the scale which reflects the precise magnitude of the sense of well-being that you are experiencing here and now. Once you've activated the Meter, please do not attempt to control or influence the needle. The Meter works very well by itself. You need only observe the needle and let it tell you what your measurement is."

Once measurements have been obtained, I ask the members to sit in a circle in rank order with the lowest self-rater sitting to my right and the highest to my left. After they have positioned themselves I divide them into several small groups. For example, if I have 24 members, I break them up into four families of six each by having them count off in order, beginning with the lowest self-rater, "one," "two," "three," "four," "one," "two," and so on. Then the "ones" meet in one part of the room; the "twos" in another location, and so forth. In this manner members are combined into families which are roughly equal with respect to their average sense of well-being. Each group has two members with high self-ratings, two with moderate ratings, and two with low ones.

After families have located themselves in their assigned areas, I say: "First obtain a group average of the sense of well-being ratings in your family. Then begin your family meeting. Remember, your aim in this meeting, individually and collectively, is to raise the level of well-being in your family as a whole. You can go about this task in many different ways. It is up to you as a group to decide what procedures you will follow. I will call time in thirty minutes, and then you will each consult your Meter and obtain a second measurement of your sense of well-being."

After thirty minutes I call time: "Please stop. Close your eyes, consult your Meters, and see what your second measurements are. Then obtain a group average of these new ratings." Once families have done this, I continue, "For the next half hour, engage in a 'post-mortem' in which you aim at achieving an understanding of what factors facilitated or interfered with raising your group average. Begin with a go-round in which each member in turn announces his first and second ratings and then gives feedback to each of the other members, being as specific as he can in letting each of them know what it was that he did or said (or didn't do or say) that had a positive or negative impact. For example, 'Jane, I was really turned off by your insisting that I tell you what was bothering me after I repeatedly made it clear that I did not feel trusting enough to do that. And, Bill, I really relaxed when you squeezed my hand and told me that you have often felt lonely too,' etc." After this go-around is completed, discuss what kinds of interventions and skills you might like to practice in future family meetings."

EVALUATION OF THE COURSE'S IMPACT

To date I have focused most of my energy on developing the course (especially family formation and communication training) and have hardly begun to study the events and dynamics of family meetings, and so there are many questions that remain to be explored as to what happens when laymen get together on their own with the avowed purpose of facilitating their own and each other's growth and with the variety of hidden agendas (including the unfinished business from their childhood families) that are part of any group's experience. When I first asked families to meet on their own I kept my fingers crossed out of concern that some participants might be "mauled," indeed "maimed" by insensitive or punitive members, but students' written evaluations of the course and their family meetings, as well as my own observations in the classroom, indicate that a majority of participants find their experiences decidedly valuable in terms of expanded self-awareness, enhanced self-esteem, and/or more satisfying, interpersonal relationships.[2] Following are examples of positive reports I have received from family members following the course's termination. I recognize that the validity, depth, and permanence of the positive influences described in these excerpts are unknown, but they do give the reader some sense of what the subjectively felt family experience is like for at least some members:

> For me this wasn't a Second Chance Family. I don't think I ever had a First Chance Family, so it was my first try at what a "family" should offer its members. It felt good when someone said, "You know, Bill, you didn't even look at me when you talked to me. Why?" It felt good because someone was actually

telling *me* that he had noticed something about *me,* and was paying attention to *me.* A strange feeling, because my entire life has been spent noticing others, paying attention to them, recognizing their individuality, serving them, pleasing them. I had just about forgotten about me—and I thank my "family" members for reminding me about myself.

"I took a risk at our last meeting and expressed what to me seems an idea of mine that sounds crazy; that is, that I am vicious, mean, and cruel, and that maybe I am not the only one who is like this, but it is common to mankind. I got the feedback that maybe this was anger that was pent up, not expressed, and came out as vicous, and if that anger was expressed appropriately, it would not come out like that. This feedback was given in a helpful and kind way, and I really valued my family for it.

Knowing that there are seven very special people who care about me, whom I care about, and whose caring I carry about with me all the time makes me feel that all in all I'm a very lucky person to have the capacity to share in this. After all, if I'm a member of this group, aren't I also pretty special? To have your craziness accepted by others, and even to be loved for it sometimes—what better way to give one a sense of life!

I remember once having a very deep wellspring being tapped, crying uncontrollably, and finally when I could bring myself to, looking around and finding that I felt a sense of home around me—and I'm crying again now remembering it.

One evening I felt very ineffective and restless in the family and decided to go home early. I said goodnight and started to put my coat on. When I left the room Jane said, "I don't know why, but it's important that we stop Mary from leaving." So the whole family came and asked me to stay, and I got very upset and insisted on going. But they said no, and I started to cry. I fell apart. And I knew that it was OK. Later when I went home I had made up my mind not to go back because I couldn't take that kind of acceptance. I knew they would respect my decision not to face things I felt I wasn't ready to deal with. Knowing that, knowing their belief in me, I returned the next week.

Those months with my family were some of the most important in my life. It was the first time I really began to see myself. Much was painful, but in seeing the fears, I was able to see my "good." I felt enormous trust in me coming from Harriet, Frank, Rose, Lennie, and Bert. With their trust and love and knowing, I was able to see—me—the ways I had of hurting myself and stopping myself. After a while together, we'd call each other on our own games. For example, if I'd say something like, "Oh, I don't know," (this is one of my old ways)—I'd follow it up with, "There I go again, saying I don't know something I know." If I didn't say it, one of my family would. "Rachel, you're doing it again. You know, and I know you know." They were always *there* for me—hearing, listening, seeing, caring.

There has been developing a groundswell of new forms of communal living in our culture, reflecting a yearning among increasing numbers for a sense of intimate participation in a small group where one can be one's self with minimum facade or armor. Most communal experiments apparently end in failure. This suggests that the achievement of productive intimacy in groups requires much work and development in the arts of communication and self-confrontation, and that courses such as the second chance family can make a contribution by offering training in the assimilation of attitudes and skills that transcend our self-defeating conditionings.

NOTES

1. This exercise was inspired by the "think-and-listen" sessions of reevaluation counseling (Jackins, 1973).

2. Evidence is mounting that leaderless groups can be productive (Beach, 1968; Berzon et al., 1968; Gibb and Gibb, 1968; Solomon and Berzon, 1969), and nonprofessionals can be trained to be effective change agents (Guerney, 1969; Jackins, 1973).

REFERENCES

ASSAGIOLI, R. (1965) Psychosynthesis: A Manual of Principles and Techniques. New York: Hobbs, Dorman.

BEACH, L. R. (1968) Learning and Student Interaction in Small Self-directed College Groups. Final Report, Project No. 7E-020 Grant, U.S. Department of Health, Education, and Welfare. Holland, Mich.: Hope College.

BERZON, B., N. N. SOLOMIN, and J. I. REISEL (1968) Self-directed Small Group Programs: A New Resource in Rehabilitation. Final Narrative Report on Vocational Rehabilitation Administration Project RD-1748. La Jolla, Calif.: Western Behavioral Sciences Institute.

ELLIS, A. and R. A. HARPER (1961) A Guide to Rational Living. Englewood Cliffs, N.J.: Prentice-Hall.

GIBB, J. R. and L. M. GIBB (1968) "Leaderless groups: growth-centered values and potentialities," in H. Otto and J. Mann (eds.) Ways of Growth. New York: Grossman.

GUERNEY, B. G., Jr. (1969) Psychotherapeutic Agents: New Roles for Non-Professionals, Parents, and Teachers. New York: Holt, Rinehart & Winston.

HARRIS, T. A. (1969) I'm OK—You're OK: A Practical Guide to Transactional Analysis. New York: Harper & Row.

JACKINS, H. (1973) The Human Situation. Seattle: Rational Island.

MALAMUD, D. I. (1974) "Self-confrontation in the second chance family." J. of Humanistic Psychology 14 (Spring)

——— (1973) "The god exercise: a self-confrontation technique." Voices 9 (Summer): 24-28.

——— (1972) "The second chance family: training adults in self-confrontation." J. of Contemporary Psychotherapy 5 (Winter): 35-39.

——— (1971) "The second chance family: a medium for self-directed growth," in M. Gottesgen et al. (eds.) Confrontation: Encounters in Self and Interpersonal Awareness. New York: Macmillan.

——— (1969) "The workshop in self-understandig: group techniques in self-controntation," pp. 245-255 in M. Ruitenbeek (ed.) Group Therapy Today: Styles, Methods, and Techniques. New York: Atherton.

——— (1960) "Educating adults in self-understanding." Mental Hygiene 44: 115-124.

——— (1958) "A workshop in self-understanding designed to prepare patients for psychotherapy." Amer. J. Psychotherapy 12: 771-786.

——— (1955) A Participant-Observer Approach to the Teaching of Human Relations. Chicago: Center for the Study of Liberal Education for Adults.

——— and S. MACHOVER (1965) Toward Self-Understanding: Group Techniques in Self-Confrontation. Springfield, Ill.: Charles C Thomas.

PERLS, F. S. (1969) Gestalt Therapy Verbatim. Lafayette, Calif.: Real People Press.

ROGERS, C. R. (1961) On Becoming a Person. Boston: Houghton Mifflin.

SOLOMON, L. N. and B. BERZON (1969) "The self-directed group: a new direction in personal growth learning," in J. T. Hart and T. M. Tomlinson (eds.) New Directions in Client-centered Psychotherapy. Boston: Houghton Mifflin.

FAMILY COMMUNICATION SYSTEMS

LOREN BENSON
MICHAEL BERGER
WILLIAM MEASE
Human Synergistics
Bach Institute

Family members cannot not communicate with each other. Any action within the family unit, including avoidance, holds some message for other family members. Because of the pervasiveness of family communication processes no family can avoid difficulties in this area. Honest and clear communication among family members is not a static outcome which can be achieved and forgotten; it is an ongoing process which requires constant maintenance (just plain hard work) to exist, even for a majority of the time.

We do not wish to appear overly negativistic about the development of effective family communication processes; ours is a hopeful attitude. Yet we cannot afford to be less than realistic about the communication problems and their consequences which all families face. The struggles required to develop a positive family communication system can be great, but the rewards for enduring these struggles are inevitably greater.

THE CORD AND THE KNOT

One of the difficulties evident when viewing communication within the family as a system is that no family member can stand outside of the family and act as an objective observer. The interdependence of family members is evidenced by the tremendous personal involvement they demonstrate when acting with or reacting to others in the family. It is this personal involvement, not made by choice, but implicit in the nature of the family, which makes it difficult for us as family members to be aware of the consistent effects other members have on us and we on them.

The prime difficulty in untangling the knot of our own family communication problems arises from the fact that we, all of us, are the cords in the knot we are attempting to disentangle. Continually unraveling the knot requires help from a source outside of the family system itself and commitment from somewhere within that system. It is our belief that a developmental, educational approach to family communication can be an effective outside source of aid in creating and maintaining positive communication systems within the family.

LOOKING BACKWARD

The phrase, "you can't choose your parents," probably holds more import than most of us are willing to admit. Each of us enters a family without being able to choose its creators, and with no control over the conditions in the family existing prior to our birth. From this completely other-determined soil springs the experience upon which our own present and future relationships will depend. Satir (1972: 24) describes the impact the family has on each child:

> Any infant, coming in the world has no past, no experience in handling himself, no skill by which to judge his own worth. He must rely on the experiences he has with people around him and

the messages they gave him about his worth as a person. For the first five or six years the child's self-esteem is formed by the family almost exclusively. After he starts school other influences come into play, but the family effect remains throughout his adolescence. Outside forces tend to reinforce the feelings of self-worth or worthlessness that he learned at home. The high self-esteem child can weather many failures in school among peers. The low self-esteem child can experience many successes and yet feel a gnawing doubt about his own value.

We develop not only certain feelings of self-esteem, but techniques of relating to others through our family origin. Most important, they affect two major problem areas which arise in any family: (1) how marriage partners express and meet each other's needs, and (2) how parents give the kind of input to their children that facilitates the development of positive self-esteem.

MEETING MY NEEDS—MEETING YOUR NEEDS

Understanding our own and another's world, knowing the ingredients required to meet our own and another's needs, demands in all of its awesome simplicity-complexity an awareness of the relationship systems in which both yourself and the other are currently involved. It is the purpose of a systems approach to family communication to create an awareness of the similar effects of what appear to be dissimilar communications. Thus, family and relationship problems which appear dissimilar on the surface can be traced to a pervasive communication system which is creating negative feelings. Recognition and/or change of this core element is a basic ingredient in the maintenance and development of healthy families.

YOUR CHILD'S FEELINGS ABOUT HIMSELF

A child entering an existing family system is dependent upon a blueprint of which neither parent is totally aware. It is a blueprint which, nevertheless, is designed to insure his survival and growth. The child is in no other position than to absorb what he is fed . . . no less than his parents absorbed from their parents. His information processing capabilities are limited, but his range of feelings is not. Given this imbalance certain distortions in his perceptions are inevitable. However, one point is clear: it is the parents' input which is paramount in the development of his feelings of self and self in relation to others. Unfortunately, this input itself may be difficult for both child and parents to understand.

A major thrust of our program, "Family Communication Systems," is to teach parents to be clear about the source of their feedback, be it their own feelings, characteristics of the situation, or a specific behavior of the child. These skills are crucial in that they clarify the data upon which the child's development of self-esteem rests. It is part of a preventative approach, the outcomes of which involve the highest of stakes—the positive development of a child.

SOME ADULT CONSEQUENCES OF THE SELF-IMAGE OF THE CHILD

The low self-esteem person is unable to develop a relationship in which control is shared. This can be viewed as the result of the negative communication systems he experienced and learned in his family of origin. He is unable to develop positive feelings about himself in relation to others. This, too, is an outcome of experiencing only "blocking" communication systems in the family. In the program, Family Communication Systems, four basic "blocking" systems and one "open" system are identified. Awareness of these five systems is a crucial beginning step in avoiding the negative adult consequences of low self-esteem in children.

CONTENT: A VEHICLE FOR SENDING RELATIONSHIP MESSAGES

As mentioned previously, a major benefit of a system approach to family communication is that it facilitates identification of a core element to which many superficially dissimilar communication problems may be attributed. This is tied to the important distinction made in this program between content and process. It is posited that every relationship system consists of "the attitudes each individual has about himself and the attitudes each has about the other" (Mease and Hollinbeck, 1971: D-1). It is the communication of these attitudes which determines the outcomes of control and self-other feelings in the relationship. These attitudes are labeled as "counting" or "not counting" in the relationship. They are presented in any significant interaction, but they are most often not communicated directly. They are process elements. As explained (by Mease and Hollinbeck, 1972: D-5):

> We don't generally walk up to each other and say, "I'd like to have a relationship with you in which I count and you don't count." or "I don't want to count in this relationship, but I'd like to control you." We communicate these attitudes indirectly by using the content of the particular situation we are in.

For example, parents may tell their children how ineffective they are through negative statements about the friends they decide to be with, the clothes they choose to wear, or the way they behave at grandma's house. Although the content of each communication is different the process is the same—that of transmitting the attitude to the child that he does not count. We have developed the concept of a "situation machine" to emphasize that the content of an infinite number of situations can be used to deliver the same process message in terms of control and feelings of counting or not counting.

It is this emphasis on differentiating the process of sending relationship messages from the situational or content components of a given communication which, when coupled with the adjustment skills of sending clear positive and negative messages to children, can aid both parents and children in their growth as individuals and as a family unit.

THE NEED FOR A DEVELOPMENTAL PROGRAM

It has become increasingly evident to us that our society will not solve its ever-growing mental health problems by waiting for serious psychological disorders to occur. We feel that developmental activity dealing with family systems is one very effective preventative intervention available to those in the pupil services area. By providing parents with the techniques for loosening the knots that are inevitable in any family system, we can reduce the crises which students and their families experience.

Examination of the need for this type of program discloses that little or no assistance in child-rearing practices has been provided for parents. Parent training is most generally made up of the parent's own experience in his family of origin, an abundance of contradictory statements in various advice columns, and an occasional course in child psychology.

Numerous studies and expert opinions clearly focus on the fact that parents need help in their parenting skills. Blum (1972) of the Stanford Institute for Policy Analysis states in his recent book:

> When illicit drug use exceeds its normal experimental or social norms, and becomes a devious means for communicating rebellion or hostility or for emotional escape, then a pathological situation probably exists within the family.

Westley and Epstein (1969) tie the mental health of children to the communication skills of their parents. Corkville [Briggs] (1972) states: "We parents are not trained for our job. Vast sums are spent to teach academic and vocational skills, but the art of becoming a nurturing parent is left to chance and a few scattered classes. And yet, paradoxically, we regard children as our most important resource."

Many other sources could be cited, all stating how important the family is to a child's feeling of self-worth. Yet, how inadequate is current preparation for the development of effective families?

A DEVELOPMENTAL PROGRAM FOR PARENTS

The material above is a general summary of concerns and assumptions which led us at Human Synergistics to develop our Family Communication Systems program. Although the program itself does not deal directly with identifying relationship systems indigenous to the family of origin, it does so indirectly by bringing about an awareness of current relationship systems of participants. Parents learn the effects of five different relationship systems which range in their outcomes from single to shared control and from feelings of worthlessness about self and hostility toward another to feelings of mutual respect in which each individual counts.

Our program's basic method of teaching parents to make active interventions in relationships stresses experiencing these interventions with someone other than their spouse in role-playing situations. This gives parents an opportunity to practice alternative methods of relating in a context which has less emotional commitment than does a family relationship.

Looking at alternative systems in a nonthreatening setting enables parents to choose different modes of relating to each other and their children. Through reading in the "Parent Handbook" and extensive experiential training, parents learn to make active interventions in their current relationship systems. These interventions are aimed at developing relationships of shared control in which all parties feel as though they and the other "count."

THE POSITIVE SIDE

Almost all parents intend to help their children grow into mentally healthy adults. Thus, parents are eager to increase their skills in this area. It is communication and behavior adjustment skills to use with their children, not the desire to be "good" parents, which they lack. Given a variety of skills from which to choose they are eager to facilitate their children's development. Of import to many, they find that they can incorporate some of these alternative ways of parenting within the value system they prize.

PROGRAM CONTENT

Facilitative listening: being sensitive to both the content and the feeling of what a child or spouse has to say. The objective is to help the child "own" his problem by helping him clarify his thoughts and feelings as he works toward a solution.

Goal setting: a bridge between awareness and application of new ideas and skills. The objective is to increase the actual application of what has been learned by increasing the specificity of the situation in which it will be initially attempted.

Identification of parenting styles: recognition of one's current mode of parenting and its effect on the child. This is seen as a precondition for the improvement of parenting.

Sending negative feelings: being able to express negative feelings in a way in which the child will not feel totally rejected. Parents are guided toward legitimate expression of their negative feelings, tying these feelings to a specific behavior of the child, and moving with the child toward a behavior which might satisfactorily take the place of the undesirable behavior.

Sending positive feelings: appropriate reinforcement of behavior which parents wish their children to maintain or increase. The objective is to create an atmosphere where all family members can realistically accept the praise and affection of others.

Systems analysis skills: ways of identifying repetitive behavior patterns in the family which leave given individuals feeling as though they count or do not count in relationship to other family members. The objective is to enable parents to change systems they feel are having a negative effect on their children or their marital relationship.

Creative problem solving: effective use of the previous skills within a framework which allows input from all family members and leads to effective decision-making in matters concerning the entire family.

Family rules: an awareness of hidden rules which are behind unsatisfactory behavior within the family. The objective is to first identify the rules which have negative effects and then develop strategies for changing these to more effective, positive rule structures.

Experiential learning activities based upon the above have been structured into a seven-evening program. In addition, a parent handbook has been developed which follows the content presented in each unit and provides the parents with reinforcing activities to help them integrate the concepts they have experienced in the session.

During the sessions there is much use of role-playing in structured situations to provide each participant with personal awareness and new alternatives to use within his own family.

RESEARCH RESULTS

The following five tables show the breakdown of the data gained from the Herford Parent Attitude Survey (Herford,

1963). The five areas covered in the survey were developed by a subcommittee of the research counsel and were based on a triple prerequisite of the area being important to parent-child relationships, measurable, and receptive to influence by educational methods. The five areas concerning parental attitudes are:

(1) confidence in parental role, referring to the parent's concept of himself ranging from inadequate feelings to adequate in meeting the demands of parenthood;

(2) causation of the child's behavior; this scale is concerned with how a parent sees himself as a causative factor relating to his child's behavior. At one end of the continuum is the parent who believes his child's behavior is inherited, at the other end is a parent who feels his child's behavior is determined by parent-child interaction, by environmental factors, and by parental behavior and attitudes;

(3) acceptance of the child's behavior and feelings. This scale measures the degree to which a parent is satisfied with his child's behavior. He or she sees the child as an individual at one end of the continuum as a rejected object; at the other end is the extremely permissive parent;

(4) mutual understanding is the fourth parent scale. This scale is based on communication with the variable at the lower end of this continuum indicating the parent who does not share ideas, attitudes, or feelings with his child; at the upper end is the parent who believes in the reciprocal exchange of both the intellectual and emotional aspects of living;

(5) mutual trust is the fifth scale. This scale measures the amount of confidence that parents and children have in each other. At the lower end of this continuum is a parent-child relationship marked by suspicion and deceit; at the other end is a relationship characterized by mutual confidence or trust.

The following tables show a comparison of experimental and control, pre- and post-mean scores, standard deviation, post-t scores, n's, and degrees of freedom (n-1). The test

TABLE 1
PARENTS' CONFIDENCE SCALE

	Pretest		Posttest	
	Experimental	Control	Experimental	Control
$\bar{X}$	57.889	58.889	61.467	57.722
SD	6.048	4.269	5.397	6.182
t			3.166[b]	.699116
n	18	18	18	18
df. (n-1)	17	17	17	17

NOTE: H_0: for the experimental group of $\mu_1 = \mu_2$ was rejected; t = 3.1663.
a. $\sigma.05$.
b. $\sigma.01$.
c. $t > 2.11$.

statistic used was a t-test matched pair formula. A critical point of 2.11 was used to determine statistical significance. The null hypotheses were: (1) there is no significant difference between the means of the pre- and post-experimental groups; (2) there is no significant difference between the means of the pre- and post-control groups. These two hypotheses were examined for each of the five scales listed above. These data are reported in Tables 1-5.

TABLE 2
PARENTS' CAUSATION SCALE

	Pretest		Posttest	
	Experimental	Control	Experimental	Control
$\bar{X}$	64.994	65.833	69.467	65.33
SD	6.566	4.630	5.083	4.550
t			4.97657[b]	.35287
n	18	18	18	18
df. (n-1)	17	17	17	17

NOTE: H_0: for the experimental group of $\mu_1 = \mu_2$ was rejected; t = 4.97657.
a. $\sigma.05$.
b. $\sigma.01$.
c. $t > 2.11$.

TABLE 3
PARENTS' ACCEPTANCE SCALE

	Pretest		Posttest	
	Experimental	Control	Experimental	Control
$\overline{X}$	61.11	65.00	65.533	63.944
SD	5.368	5.087	6.300	3.918
t			3.38582[b]	.864174
n				
df. (n-1)	17	17	17	17

NOTE: H_0: for experimental group of $\mu_1 = \mu_2$ was rejected; t = 3.38582.
a. σ.05.
b. σ.01.
c. t > 2.11.

It is interesting to note that on all five of the scales described the experimental group showed a statistically significant change equal to or greater than the .05 and .01 levels of confidence. The control group showed no evidence of anything but random change as indicated by the fluctuation in their t-scores. These data support our hypotheses that an educational training program in parent-child communication does have a significant influence on parent attitude in the five critical areas described already.

TABLE 4
PARENTS' UNDERSTANDING SCALE

	Pretest		Posttest	
	Experimental	Control	Experimental	Control
$\overline{X}$	63.722	61.167	66.600	62.667
SD	3.997	7.160	6.280	4.678
t			3.2645[b]	.770126
n				
df. (n-1)	17	17	17	17

NOTE: H_0: of experimental group $\mu_1 = \mu_2$ was rejected; t = 3.2645.
a. σ.05.
b. σ.01.
c. t > 2.11.

TABLE 5
PARENTS' TRUST SCALE

	Pretest		Posttest	
	Experimental	Control	Experimental	Control
X	60.944	60.11	64.20	61.778
SD	6.557	7.903	8.196	8.565
t			2.56862[a]	.950072
n	18	18	18	18
df. (n-1)	17	17	17	17

NOTE: H_0: of experimental group $\mu_1 = \mu_2$ was rejected; t = 2.56862.
SOURCE: Berger and Haversack, 1973.
a. 0.05.
b. 0.01.
c. t > 2.11.

A study by Campion (1973: 57) comparing an Adelerian-Gordon model to the Family Communication Systems model showed the following results on the Herford-Parent Attitude Survey and on the family questionnaire (an instrument developed for this study): the experimental groups improved significantly more on the PAS scales measuring confidence, causation, and understanding. The scores on the acceptance and trust scale did not show a significant difference between experimental and control groups. The data obtained from the family questionnaire supported the hypothesis that participation in either parent education group would produce significantly improved communication patterns when compared to control groups. The Family Communication System group improved significantly more than did the Adelerian-Gordon group on the family questionnaire.

COMMENTS BY PARENTS

The following comments made by parents about the Family Communication Systems program gave more credence to our assumption that parents are willing and eager to gain new skills in the art of parenting.

"Our children are telling us more about events in their lives."

"My husband and I are able to talk to each other in a clearer way about our relationship."

"The problem solving methods helped our family to do a better job of organizing household duties."

"I noticed that the children are using the listening skills and that we don't have the usual confusion while discussing things at the dinner table."

"The DESI and DEE messages have been effective in changing my child's sassy remarks."

These are but a few of the overwhelming number of positive comments we have received about the Family Communication Systems program.

This program has been used not only by social workers, psychologists, and counselors in schools but also by leaders in drug abuse centers, social service agencies, and churches. It has been used effectively both in developmental programs and programs addressed to special needs such as the parenting of children with special learning and behavior problems, hearing impairment, and retardation.

The authors have formed a corporation to offer the program services described in this article. The thrust of their Family Communication Systems training programs is to prepare professionals to conduct a series of experientially oriented (about 70% of the total time) learning activities that they in turn can use with parent groups of 10-18 people.

NOTE

Additional information may be obtained by writing the authors: Human Synergistics, c/o Bach Institute, 628 Nicollet Mall, Minneapolis, Minnesota, 55402; phone (612) 339-1777. A copy of the Parent Handbook is now available from Human Synergistics.

REFERENCES

BERGER, M. and L. BENSON (1973) Family Communication Systems: An Instructor's Manual. Minneapolis, Minn.: Human Synergistics.
BERGER, M. and D. HAVERSACK, (1973) "Improving Family Communication Systems," in D. Miller (ed.) Additional Studies in Elementary School Guidance: Psychological Education Activities Evaluated. Minnesota Department of Education.
BLUM, R. (1972) Horatio Alger's Children. San Francisco: Jossey-Bass.
CAMPION, S. (1973) "A Comparison of Two Parent Education Models," in D. Miller (ed.) Additional Studies in Elementary School Guidance: Psychological Education Activities Evaluated. Minnesota Department of Education.
CORKVILLE, D. (1972) Your Child's Self-Esteem. Garden City, N.Y.: Doubleday.
HERFORD, C. F. (1963) Changing Parental Attitude Through Group Discussion. Austin: Univ. of Texas Press.
MEASE, W. and R. HOLLINBECK (1971) Family Communication Systems Developmental Activities for Parents. Minneapolis, Minn.: Human Synergistics.
SATIR, V. (1972) Peoplemaking. Palo Alto: Science Behavior Books.
WESTLEY, W. A. and N. B. EPSTEIN (1969) The Silent Majority. San Francisco: Jossey-Bass.

BECOMING US
An Experiment in Family Learning and Teaching

PATRICK J. CARNES
Chemical Dependency Specialist Training Program
Metropolitan Community College, Minneapolis
HERBERT LAUBE
Program for Sexuality
University of Minnesota Medical School

Twelve years ago Hobart (1963) wrote:

> There are many attempts to characterize the nature of modern society: the affluent society, ... the pluralistic society, the achieving society, the insane society. Most of these characterizations share at least one underlying assumption, that as a society we tread where man has never trod before, that there are qualitative differences between our society and earlier ones which make extrapolation on the basis of earlier societal experience unreliable at best, and often completely invalid.

> It must be admitted that the family is undergoing changes, both within itself and in relation to the rest of society, which tend to significantly weaken its solidarity. At least four of these changes may be mentioned: (1) loss of functions; (2) increased personal mobility within society; (3) the decline of status ascription, and the increase in status achievement; and (4) the ascendency of materialistic values.

Similarly, Lewis (1971) notes six areas in which societal and familial systems of values lead to strains:

(1) Strains relating to competitive practices among individuals within the family and in individual-societal contacts;

(2) Strains relating to the preservation of strong kinship ties and the maintenance of larger kinship units;

(3) Strains relating to social control and stable kinship authority structures;

(4) Strains relating to changing role definitions for women;

(5) Strains relating to the transmission of culture;

(6) Strains relating to the development and maintenance of emotional intimacy.

Over the past five years additional changes have been witnessed particularly in terms of a sudden mushrooming of youth-oriented services; drop-in centers, telephone counseling services, "crash pads" in schools, runaway houses, VD clinics—all of these may be seen as failsafe systems to deal with breakdowns in family functioning (Skolnick, 1973). Along with this development there has been heightened interest and the emergence of: new family forms (White House Conference on Children, 1970, Report of Forum 14), parent effectiveness training (Gordon, 1970), family counseling workshops and institutes, and family clusters proposals (Stoller, 1970; Sawin, 1971; Otto, 1963; Pringle, 1974). In the context of this change we are developing a family communication problem-solving program called Becoming Us to assist families: (1) to learn listening and speaking skills, (2) to clarify what values they have as individuals and as a family unit, (3) to learn effective problem-solving skills.

In addition to these skills the program is designed to provide enrichment (in terms of emotional intimacy) by improving the families' ability to deal with affect as well as to encourage them to focus on nonverbal dimensions of their interaction. This enrichment process can be considered a significant socialization process since we live in a time of rising psychological expectations (Yarburg, 1973) and increased awareness of and desire for intimacy (Skolnick, 1973).

THEORETICAL DISCUSSION

Some of the assumptions of the Becoming Us program are that it is designed: (1) for so-called "normal families"; it is not intended to be a therapy program; (2) as a preventative for serious problems; it is not intended to be a remedial program; (3) as an experience-based (dynamic-process oriented) program (necessitated, in part, by including young children)—it is not an academic or intellectual program (static-content focused) about a generalized American family; (4) for developing communication problem-solving skills; it is not designed to discuss the importance of communication problem-solving abilities; (5) to enrich and deepen the family's interaction; it is not a "sensitivity" program in which confrontation is the focus.

The program is based primarily upon modern systems theory. Other theories which contribute to the program come from family therapy, social learning theory, and humanistic psychology. A family can be considered to be a complex system. Buckley (1967) defines a system as follows: "A system is a complex of elements or components directly or indirectly related in a causal network such that each component is related to at least some other in a more or less stable way within any particular time period." One component of a system, then, is that its elements are interdependent. Any change in one element has an effect upon other elements. In terms of the family this means that the elements, or positions (mother-wife, father-husband, daughter-sister, son-brother) are to varying degrees interdependent. Any change by one person will affect every other person (Aldous, 1967). Hence the program examines various "parent" and "kid" styles of interrelating. For example, if the father is a "dictator," their child might be a "rebel" or a "placator." The dominant style for the parent usually shapes the style of the child—the styles are interacting and mutually reinforcing.

Because all elements of a system (family) are interdependent, the Becoming Us program has been designed so that all the members of the family are present at the training sessions. Working with all of the family simultaneously follows a pattern which has been utilized by many family therapists. Although the program focus is educational rather than therapeutic, the greatest effort in applying systems theory to the family has been done by family therapists. A brief historical excursion will highlight some key components to this development.

According to Zuk (1971) the major trend which has occurred from 1964-1970 appears to be a deepening and broadening of the struggle between the advocates of an individual-oriented family therapy based on the psychoanalytic therapists' focus on the dyad of therapist and patient— and those advocating a systems approach which focuses on triads—units of three (sometimes more) including a therapist and two family members. In the psychoanalytic model the identified patient is seen as the problem in the family and consequently the effort by the therapist is to delve into the patient's history and "unconscious processes." In contrast to this the systems approach sees the identified patient as a symptom of a problem family, and consequently the therapist attempts to bargain or negotiate with the family to bring about change. Boszormenyi-Nagy, Satir, Wynne, Jackson, and Bowen have utilized systems theory. Others who have been developing the systems approach are McGregor et al. (1964; multiple impact theory), Watzlawick et al. (1967; behavioral effects of human communication), and Brodey (1968; flow of human interaction—cybernetic concepts to understanding family processes).

The key implications for an educational program from family therapists are that in order to alleviate pathology and promote health of family members, it is important to work with: (1) dyads and triads rather than individuals; (2) a whole system in order to "heal" the identified patient; and (3) the communication pattern of the system.

Another component of the family as a system is that it is a task performance group meeting demands of other societal agencies as well as those of its members (Aldous, 1967). This is a complex process. The family has many tasks to be performed. Working out a plan for task allocation occurs in every family either implicitly or explicitly. Skill in decision-making and problem-solving are needed so that smoother task performance can be realized.

Social learning theory provides explanation as to how parents and children go about the normal process of changing each other (Patterson, 1971). Much behavior which occurs in the family represents the outcome of what we have learned from other people. Two key processes from social learning theory which indicate how learning occurs are: (1) positive reinforcement and (2) social imitation. Positive reinforcement entails the use of rewards to increase the strength of a response tendency. Both pro-social and problem behaviors can be reinforced positively. Social imitation is a process in which one person imitates the behavior of another person; it involves learning an amazing variety of behaviors including when to smile, what and how to communicate, how to express affection, and the like.

The humanistic psychology perspective is evidenced in our program as follows: (1) Centering of attention on worth of experiencing person and his uniqueness. Sessions are dynamically designed so that each person experiences direct learning interaction with his family members; each family member is encouraged to individually relate directly to every other member of his family during the program. (2) Emphasizing distinctively human qualities of choice, creativity, and self-realization. Each person chooses with whom he will interact during various experiences; persons are encouraged to relate as persons rather than role-to-role: for example, father to son in fixed stereotyped roles, father always disciplinarian and son always disciplined (Buckland, 1972). This program particularly builds upon Satir's books, *Conjoint Family Therapy* (1964), *Peoplemaking* (1972), Otto's (1963) article, "Criteria for Assessing Family Strength," and positive reinforcement (Bandura and Walters, 1963). Satir and Otto capitalize on healthy potential in families in contrast to many therapists who focus mainly on pathology.

Of parallel importance to the theoretical base of the program has been research in the areas of values development such as the research of Simon et al. (1966), Rokeach (1973), and Kohlberg (1971), and conscience formation. Especially important has been the cognitive developmental framework of Kohlberg, whose extensive longitudinal and transcultural studies indicate a common sequence of stages in personal moral development. Kohlberg's stages of moral judgment were the basic model for a singularly important study for this project done by Holstein (1969).

Key findings of the Holstein study are that families which tended to have children at higher stages on the Kohlberg scale were families which also: (1) spent more time in discussing moral and value-related issues; (2) encouraged participation by children in family decision-making; and (3) established an environment which encouraged give and take between adult and child. It is interesting to note that other researchers have made similar links between these factors and the development of self-concept (Baumrind, 1971).

Central to the Becoming Us approach, therefore, is the establishing of a supportive environment, involving young people in family decision-making and structuring time for families to talk about their values.

HISTORY AND DEVELOPMENT OF PROGRAM

The initial development for Becoming Us began in the fall of 1972 with a local grant from the Minnesota Conference of the United Church of Christ. Our mandate was to design a family enrichment program to be used ecumenically by local churches. The alliance with the churches has been most fortuitous due to their intense interest as well as their credibility. Our access into the community has been assisted a great deal by church support.

The first program was piloted in the spring of 1973 as an eight-session program and was taught by professional staff. After the initial pilot program and additional funding, materials were modified and trainer-families were selected from the participants of the first pilot program. The role of the trainer-family was to be an instructional team in Becoming Us groups. The assumption was that families as instructional teams could provide modeling, credibility, and accessibility far beyond that of a "professional" staff. The program was successfully piloted again with trainer-families as instructor-facilitators. Currently, the staff focuses its energies in training "trainer-families" and developing and evaluating the program.

This process has been rich in learning about the practical implementation of family-centered programs. One of the most significant outcomes has been the realization that an extremely important value of the program is that it provided a structured time for families to work on their relationships. Families indicated that their lives together were so fragmented that there was little opportunity for any real sharing. A by-product of the actual skill training was that the program built in time for family members to rediscover each other and to say those things there never seemed time to say. Even if there was nothing to be learned from all the skills the training, the family self-discovery was worth the personal investment. A major goal of the program was to provide the structure, skills, and time for sharing.

To meet this goal we had to give up many of our assumptions about the most appropriate curriculum for families. Our first surprise was that there was no need for separate sessions for the parents who we thought would want more complex theoretical presentations. The young people were quite capable of picking up what we were asking of them. In fact, because of their intense interest their attention spans were capable of handling longer sessions than we had scheduled. As a result the parent sessions became unnecessary rehersals. Whatever abstract knowledge we wished to communicate to adults could be accomplished through a manual that each participating family receives at the beginning of the program.

The eliminating of the parent sessions also enabled the staff to focus on another design problem, the integration of theoretical input into the total family session. By concentrating theoretical input for the parent sessions, we did not integrate the goals and concepts into the family sessions so that learning could evolve naturally and logically. Sometimes we had the impression that people were having a good time, but that they were not sure why we were doing specific activities. The conceptual flow of the program improved by eliminating the parent sessions and integrating theoretical input into the program structure.

In terms of process, a key factor in designing more coherence into the program was the need for a common pattern in presentation. Our experience helped us to refine a basic pattern out of what worked best in the sessions. It is composed of three elements, verbalization, experience, and process.

Verbalization. A short five-to-eight-minute presentation is made on a specific concept sometimes followed by a role play or "modeling" by the staff. Our strategy involves making a helpful skill or behavior clear by surfacing those actions which are not helpful. An example would be demonstrating obstacles to listening (e.g. preaching and moralizing) before talking about appropriate modes of listening.

Experience. After each verbalization, a structured experience that the family can do together is presented to illustrate the point. The main goals of these experiences are to build specific skills, to create awareness about the concept involved, and to provide another opportunity for the family to share.

Process. As the families finish each experience, they are asked to share what their learnings were in the large group. Usually this takes the form of asking what was helpful or what was not. Sometimes an unusual surprise or amusing anecdote is reported. There seems to be a high need for families to talk about their experiences. From a staff viewpoint this process section serves to reiterate the point made in the initial verbalization. It also allows for an additional goal, to provide the opportunity for young and old to see how other families operate through this sharing.

In addition, a specific effort at the beginning and end of each program is necessary to fit together the overarching concepts. We became especially aware that processing at the session's end was insufficient to provide real closure. Some more marked experience was necessary. We found that a celebrative effort (such as singing) was well received.

An additional element that became crucial concerning format was the homework. The task of generating homework appropriate for all the different age groups that might be represented in a given family on a specific topic proved to be a monumental task. Initially, we attacked the problem as most of our colleagues have done with adults, by using a paper and pencil (cognitive) approach. The assumption, that by writing down and practicing specific responses participants would build skill, proved false. The procedure was one of the weakest elements of the program and reinforced our conviction that people (and families) learn more from experience than from intellectual input.

Currently, for each session a participating family is required to do a major homework or exercise such as constructing a family banner and writing a family "credo." In addition, there is a large number of optional events—adventures or activities designed to appeal to different interests—that families may create for themselves. These range from interfamily want ads to advertise specific personal needs, to reading "The Devil and Daniel Webster" by Stephen Vincent Benet as a family, to get a unique perspective on personal contracts. What most impressed us was the conscientious and creative efforts put into family projects. In our evaluations there was the consistent observation that homework was a valued part of the program.

Ultimately the program was reorganized around five basic sessions which reflect the fundamentals a family must have to function well:

(1) Listening to Others. This session starts with an introduction to the goals, expectations, and procedures of the course. The major focus, however, of the session is on relationships and how well we really hear what other members of the family say to us.

(2) Speaking for Myself. The goal of this session is how do I send messages about myself that accurately reflect what is going on inside me.

(3) Sharing of Values. Questions about how values and consciences are formed as well as what specifically are some of the values of our families are explored in this session.

(4) Problem-Solving. Specific techniques are practiced that families can use to solve problems based on their own values.

(5) Contracting. Once solutions are found, a specific plan of action must be developed which provides for clear responsibility as to who is going to do what. Contracting is one effective way of clarifying expectations.

The rationale for the programming is rooted in a fundamental concept which links relationships, value formation, and problem-solving. One of the key factors in developing a value is that values are determined to a great extent by one's relationships and especially by one's family relationships. In turn, the facility with which one solves problems and makes decisions is determined by knowledge of personal priorities (i.e., one's values). Finally, no solutions can work unless the implementation can be "negotiated" by the family members (hence a contract is necessary).

Each family receives a manual which contains specific inputs for each session, appropriate articles and bibliographies, materials to be used in each session, and homework materials. Each training family will have a course manual with step-by-step instructions for each session as well as recommendations and suggestions for presentations and overall coordination.

In addition to the basic five sessions, the staff has developed a series of two to three follow-up session units around specific topics. The three topics we have chosen are religious values, sexuality, and family life-style. Therefore, a church may elect, for example, to offer to families who have already gone through the five basic sessions a further series in religious values.

Perhaps one of the most gratifying and unique features of the program has been the use of the whole family as a training unit. There is an excitement and credibility that is not as available to "professional" staff who do not have their children present. The young people of trainer-families have proved invaluable resources in terms of providing their own insight, role-playing, and modeling. An unexpected turn of events has been the concept of team-teaching families. Two families that work together planning, teaching, and evaluating the sessions have proved eminently successful. A special dividend has been the growth and closeness of these trainer-families as they work together.

One of the greatest areas of concern, however, has been the training and selection of trainer-families. (To approach these problems we are using strategies involving program design as well as training.) Specifically, in the area of program design we emphasize that this is exclusively an education program to instruct the families in the use of specific skills together. It is not adequate for nor intended to provide therapy or remedial action. Families did report to us that significant problems were resolved in their families because of the program, but that was not the intended goal. In addition, the program is designed in a highly structured manner so that each session is programmed and can be taught in almost cookbook fashion without reducing program impact. Yet we encourage the flexibility to plan sessions which take into account the experience and resources of the trainer-family as well as the context. We discovered that there is a self-selection process; families that asked to be trainer-families were often the same families the staff would have chosen. We are asking of each family that they participate in training sessions wherein they will intensively go through the program again and "practice teach" its components. After the sessions each family co-teaches an entire program with a staff member to give them further confidence and experience and to provide us with one more check on the family's ability.

Another lesson for the staff has been that as an individual has a self-concept, so an entire family has a shared family concept—or a common understanding of how the individuals of the family perceive themselves as a unit or group. In fact, the idea of promoting the "shared family concept" is the overarching theme of the program; hence, it is titled Becoming Us. It focuses on the values that all members identify with and builds on commonly perceived strengths. Most importantly, it provides a time structure and process to develop contact within family. Given the stresses placed on the postindustrial family outlined in the theoretical section, it is an appropriate place to focus.

PROGRAM EVALUATION

As a program designed for total family growth, the project has raised interesting questions and fascinating possibilities. No issue has been harder to grapple with, however, than the problems of evaluation and assessment. To measure the total growth of units of varying sizes, whose members range in age from preschool to adult, on such variables as values, skills, and shared family concept is an enticing task. Heretofore, our energies have been consumed by gathering data on specific activities and materials. As the program progresses we are implementing more longitudinal approaches.

The evaluation input so far has come from the staff, the training families, and participant families. It has involved both written evaluations and in-depth interviewing including children as well as adults. This approach has been crucial to the revision of materials and program components. Within the more global aspects of the program participants report they are most appreciative of: (1) involving the whole family; (2) structuring a time to be together through sessions and homework; and (3) being led through the experience by a family just like themselves.

As the program grows it is being tested in rural as well as metropolitan settings and amongst different socioeconomic and cultural groups. It is a process constantly struck by the opportunities in working with entire families, especially in developing new models, family clusters, and instrumentation. (Whatever the ultimate impact of the program, we are certain that it is rooted in using the whole family as a resource for both learning and teaching.)

We are looking for trainer-families and organizations who wish to join in our adventure. Contact us by writing "Becoming Us," 1645 Summit Avenue, St. Paul, Minnesota 55105.

REFERENCES

ALDOUS, J. (1967) The Family Development Approach to Family Analysis. Minneapolis: Univ. of Minnesota Press.

BANDURA, A. (1962) "Social learning through imitation," pp. 211-269 in M. R. Jones (ed.) Nebraska Symposium on Motivation. Lincoln: Univ. of Nebraska Press.

——— and R. H. WALTERS (1963) Social Learning and Personality Development. New York: Holt, Rinehart & Winston.

BAUMRIND, D. (1971) "Current patterns of parental authority." Developmental Psychology Monograph 4, 1: Part 2.

BRODEY, W. M. (1968) Changing the Family. New York: Potter.

BUCKLAND, C. M. (1972) "Toward a theory of parent education: family learning centers in the post-industrial society." The Family Coordinator 21, 2 (April): 151-162.

BUCKLEY, W. (1967) Sociology and Modern Systems Theory. Englewood Cliffs, N.J.: Prentice-Hall.

DEUTSCH, M. and R. M. KRAUSS (1965) Theories in Social Psychology. New York: Basic Books.

HOBART, C. W. (1963) "Commitment, value conflict, and the future of the American family." J. of Marriage and Family 25 (November): 405-412.

HOLSTEIN, C. (1969) "The relation of children's moral judgment to that of their parents and to communication patterns in the family." Presented at the Biennial Meeting of the Society for Research in Child Development, Santa Monica, California (March).

INSKO, R. W. (1971) "Developing family actualization: the Frankport project." The Family Coordinator 20, 1 (November): 17-23.

JACKSON, D. D. (1965) "The study of the family." Family Process 4: 1-20.

KOHLBERG, L. and C. GILLIGAN (1971) "The adolescent as a philosopher: the discovery of the self in a postconventional world." Daedalus. (Journal of the American Academy of Arts and Sciences)

LEWIS, G. F. (1971) "American family social values and socio-cultural change." International J. of Contemporary Sociology 12, 4: 252-266.

McGREGOR, R. et al. (1964) Multiple Impact Therapy with Families. New York: McGraw-Hill.

OTTO, H. A. (1963) "Criteria for assessing family strength." Family Process 2: 329-337.

PATTERSON, G. R. (1971) Families: Applications of Social Learning to Family Life. Champaign, Ill.: Research Press.

PRINGLE, B. M. (1974) "Family clusters as a means of reducing isolation among urbanites." The Family Coordinator 23, 2 (April): 175-181.

ROKEACH, M. (1973) The Nature of Human Values. New York: Free Press.

SATIR, V. (1972) Peoplemaking. Palo Alto, Calif.: Science & Behavior.

——— (1964) Conjoint Family Therapy. Palo Alto, Calif.: Science & Behavior. (revised in 1967)

SAWIN, M. M. (1971) "Educating by family groups: a new model for religious education." Rochester, N.Y.: First Baptist Church. (mimeo)

SIMON, S. et al. (1966) Values and Teaching. Columbus, Ohio: Charles E. Merrill.

SKOLNICK, A. (1973) The Intimate Environment: Exploring Marriage and the Family. Boston: Little, Brown.

STOLLER, F. H. (1971) The Family Cluster: A Multi-Based Alternative. Beverly Hills, Calif.: Holistic Press.

——— (1970) "The intimate network of families as a new structure," pp. 145-160 in H. A. Otto (ed.) The Family in Search of a Future. New York: Appleton-Century-Crofts.

WATZLAWICK, P., J. H. BEAVIN, and D. D. JACKSON (1967) Pragmatics of Human Communication. New York: W. W. Norton.

White House Conference on Children (1970) Report to the President. Washington, D.C.: White House Conference on Children.

YARBURG, B. (1973) The Changing Family. New York: Columbia Univ. Press.

ZUK, T. (1971) Family Therapy: A Triadic-Based Approach. New York: Behavioral Publication.